Touchstones

A TEACHING ANTHOLOGY

Revised and expanded edition

MICHAEL AND PETER BENTON

Hodder & Stoughton

A MEMBER OF THE HODDER HEADLINE GROUP

A Catalogue for this title is available from the British Library

ISBN 0 340 40822 7

First published 1969
Second edition 1988
Impression number   15 14 13 12 11 10 9
Year   1998   1997   1996

Photoset by Rowland Phototypesetting Ltd, Bury St Edmunds, Suffolk.
Printed in Great Britain for Hodder & Stoughton Educational,
a division of Hodder Headline Plc, 338 Euston Road, London NW1 3BH
by Redwood Books, Trowbridge, Wiltshire

Contents

Reading, Talking, Writing

PEOPLE
Five Epitaphs:
Reading, Talking, Writing

To the Teacher

Since the first *Touchstones* series was launched there have been major changes in teaching methods and many exciting new poets writing for children have emerged. We have revised the series so that the basic concept of the 'teaching anthology' remains. This is still the most effective way of combining three key features: an up-to-date selection of poems; teaching approaches which are primarily concerned with the individual's responses; and activities —often in pairs or small groups—which will bring the poems off the page. While many of the poems in the original volumes are retained, we have been able to include a generous selection of verse from current writers. The teaching sections on 'Exploring Poems' and the activities suggested at the end of each group of poems in the 'Anthology' have been completely revised and expanded. Even so, books can only do so much; poetry lessons, in particular, depend for their success upon a sympathetic relationship between teacher and pupils. When this exists children can learn more about what language is and what language does from experiencing poetry than from any other form of language use. What is more, approached creatively—with ample opportunities for performance and individual involvement—poetry lessons can be fun for both teacher and pupils.

The pattern of our 'teaching anthology' is as follows. First, in 'Exploring Poems' (Part A), we introduce three main topics which give information about a particular aspect of poetry, illustrate by examples and engage the children in talking, reading, and writing about poems. The individual teacher is the best judge of just how and when to use this area of the book. Secondly, in the 'Anthology' (Part B), we have grouped the material so that the teacher will be able to deal with several poems, linked by some common quality of technique, subject matter, style or attitude, in any one lesson or sequence of lessons. Thirdly, at the end of each section in the 'Anthology' we have provided suggestions for encouraging the pupils to respond to the poems in a variety of ways: live performances, tape-recordings, personal writing, displays and so on. We consider that pupils should be offered the chance to experiment, to play with the words, sounds and shapes of poems in the same way that they play with paints and materials in an art lesson. Unless it is developed, such freedom can become mere licence. Teachers, therefore, will often want to help children redraft their first ideas. Ideally, the 'play' element leads to a delight in the discipline of form.

Opportunities for this kind of personal involvement offer children both a means of understanding and ways of developing a 'feel' for poems which are not only enjoyable in themselves but also provide the best foundation for a fuller appreciation of poetry in later years.

Finally, we hope it is evident from the approaches we adopt that we do not wish the books to be followed slavishly as a 'course'. Indeed, the distinction between material suited, for example, to a second as opposed to a third form must sometimes be arbitrary. Although the books are numbered from one to five and the topics and poems have been chosen to suit particular age groups, teachers will find sufficient flexibility in the arrangement to be able to select and modify the material according to their own tastes and the abilities of their pupils. We also suggest the building up of resources to complement our selections. A mini-library of slim volumes of poetry chosen by author is essential in any school; and there are hundreds of practical ideas in the following books:

Michael Benton and Geoff Fox: *Teaching Literature 9–14*, OUP
Peter Benton : *Pupil, Teacher, Poem*, Hodder & Stoughton
Sandy Brownjohn : *Does it Have to Rhyme?* Hodder & Stoughton
What Rhymes with Secret? Hodder & Stoughton
Ted Hughes : *Poetry in the Making*, Faber
Michael Rosen : *I See a Voice*, Hutchinson
Stephen Tunnicliffe : *Poetry Experience*, Methuen

PART A

Exploring Poems

WORD-PICTURES

(i) Smithereens

Do you collect things? Most people do at some time in their life. Perhaps you collect smithereens like Roger McGough does:

Smithereens

I spend my days
collecting smithereens.
I find them on buses
in department stores
and on busy pavements.

At restaurant tables
I pick up the leftovers
of polite conversation.
At railway stations
the tearful debris
of parting lovers.

I pocket my eavesdroppings
and store them away.
I make things out of them.
Nice things, sometimes.
Sometimes odd, like this.

ROGER McGOUGH

We all overhear fragments of conversations—angry, friendly, funny, polite, sad . . . Jot down any snatch of conversation that you can remember overhearing. It may be very brief and you may not recall it exactly. It doesn't matter. Write down what was said, perhaps just two or three lines, setting them out as you would a play with the speaker in the left margin and the dialogue opposite. Give an idea of the situation by adding a title—'At the bus-stop' or 'Overheard at the supermarket'. You have made an instant smithereen—or, at least, you have recalled an 'eavesdropping' that has been stored away. Roger McGough makes things out of these fragments. Try it. Add a few more bits of talk to your smithereen, only this time *invent* the conversation. Try to catch the typical phrases used by the people you have in mind so that their talk makes a word-picture.

Poems are often about things that have caught the writer's attention, maybe just for an instant. The object may not be new but the way of looking at it usually is; and when you start playing around with words and thinking about things in different ways, the results can be amusing.

Kangaroo-Kangaroo!

The kangaroo of Australia
Lives on the burning plain,
He keeps on leaping in the air
'Cos it's hot when he lands again.

SPIKE MILLIGAN

Or they can be clever word-puzzles like the poem overleaf. Share out the reading so that you hear a fresh voice for each section. You could tape record it.

Thirteen Ways of Looking at a Blackboard

I

The blackboard is clean.
The master must be coming.

II

The vigilant mosquito bites on a rising pitch.
The chalk whistles over the blackboard.

III

Among twenty silent children
The only moving thing
Is the chalk's white finger.

IV

O young white cricketers,
Aching for the greensward,
Do you not see how my moving hand
Whitens the black board?

V

A man and a child
Are one.
And man and a child and a blackboard
Are three.

VI

Some wield their sticks of chalk
Like torches in dark rooms.
I make up my blackboard
Like the face of an actor.

VII

I was of three minds
Like a room
In which there are three blackboards.

VIII
I dream.
I am an albino.

IX
I wake.
I forget a word.
The chalk snaps on the blackboard.

X
Twenty silent children
Staring at the blackboard.
On one wall of each of twenty nurseries
The light has gone out.

XI
He ambles among the white rocks of Dover,
Crushing pebbles with black boots.
He is a small blackboard
Writing on chalk.

XII
It is the Christmas holidays.
The white snow lies in the long black branches.
The black board
In the silent schoolroom
Perches on two stubby branches.

XIII
The flesh that is white
Wastes over the bones that are chalk,
Both in the day
And through the black night.

PETER REDGROVE

Are there any pictures that you do not 'see'?
Which pictures do you like best?

In groups of three or four, decide on a familiar object—a river, a
waterfall, an apple, a calculator, a planet—choose your own if you
can—and see if each of you can devise one or two different 'ways of
looking' at the object. Put them together in the best order as 'X Ways
of Looking at . . .'

7

(ii) Thumbnail sketches

One type of writing that is itself a 'way of looking' is the Japanese haiku poem. You may well know these tiny word-pictures already. They are not complicated to write. In the original Japanese, haiku are seventeen-syllable poems, the syllables being arranged 5, 7, 5 on the three lines. In translation, however, it is not always possible to keep this syllable pattern and often the translator has chosen to use rhymes instead to give the poems a definite shape, as you can see from the next poem.

The Dragonfly

The dragonfly:
his face is very nearly
only eye!

CHISOKU

Certainly, this haiku is about a 'way of looking'!

When haiku are written in English it is often satisfying to keep to the seventeen syllables. Here are two more regular haiku: the first, written by a boy of your own age, uses a comparison; the second, rhymes the first and the third lines.

Rain Haiku

Gentle summer rain;
Scratch, scratch upon the window
With its little stick.

COLIN ROWBOTHAM

The Mississippi River

Under the low grey
Winter skies water pushes
Water on its way.

KENNETH YASUDA

8

Both these thumbnail sketches do a bit more than simply giving us a 'way of looking'. What impression of the rain do you get from Colin's poem? What sense of the Mississippi do you have from the second poem?

Once you are sure you understand the arrangement of the syllables in haiku, try to write one or two of your own. The choice of subject is up to you but remember to focus on a single scene or sound or detail; perhaps just the record of a moment which you found memorable or significant. Try to work a comparison into your haiku; or to rhyme the first and last lines if this feels right for your subject.

The thoughts expressed in a poem always seem different from the thoughts we put into words each day in speaking, or even from the thoughts we write in an essay or letter. Poems do not usually explain feelings and ideas; they capture them. Another Japanese form called *tanka* is traditionally used to express strong feelings, often of a romantic nature. Technically, the form is like an extended haiku. It has 31 syllables arranged over five lines as follows: 5, 7, 5, 7, 7. Often there may be a break in the sense after the three-line haiku part, perhaps to set up a contrast with the final two lines. You can see how this works in the following poem:

High on the summit
the garden is all moonlight
the moon is golden.
More precious is the contact
of your lips in the shadow.

JORGE LUIS BORGES
(*trans. Alastair Reid*)

The next example is also a regular 31-syllable tanka, less romantic than the previous one but describing the tree as it if were a person with real feelings. It was written by a boy of your own age.

Tree

Swaying in the wind
I catch the people's attention.
I begin to wave,
They never wave back to me.
I think nobody likes me.

DOMINIC DOWELL

One easy way to write your own tanka is to build on an extension to the haiku you have written earlier. See if you can write the seven-syllable lines to fit on the end of your haiku. Your two lines may add more details to the word-picture, or provide a contrast to the haiku, or look at the subject from a different viewpoint.

These short, sketch-like poems often leave the situation and idea unexplained. The reader has to fill out the picture by thinking round the words that are given. What do you see happening here?

In a Station of the Metro

The apparition of these faces in the crowd;
Petals on a wet, black bough.

EZRA POUND

Little is actually stated, but a good deal is suggested.

What is the connection between the first line and the second?

Why does the poet use the word 'apparition'?

This poem was arrived at after a lot of hard work on a much longer version of the same idea. The poet's job was to prune away unnecessary words so that this finished poem would represent, in this sharp, uncluttered way, the experience of seeing a crowd of people in an underground station. Again, making every word contribute to the word-picture is something that you will not understand properly unless you attempt it yourself. Try to write a few lines which capture vividly and precisely any scene that sticks in your mind: it might be a sunset or a gasworks. Whatever you choose, when you have a first draft of, say, five or six lines, try cutting away the unnecessary lines or phrases until you have two or three lines which say just what you want. You may well try to use a comparison as Ezra Pound has done.

(iii) Changing pictures

You will already be familiar with the fact that poets often convey what they see and feel by use of comparisons. Similarly, when a poet wants to express his thoughts, he may well compare one idea with another, or present several ideas in one poem because they have something in common. Read the following poem carefully and, *on your own*, jot down any words, phrases or lines that stand out for whatever reason—perhaps because you like them, perhaps because you don't understand them. Does the poem set any thoughts or feelings going as you re-read it?

Nothing Gold Can Stay

Nature's first green is gold,
Her hardest hue to hold.
Her early leaf's a flower;
But only so an hour.
Then leaf subsides to leaf.
So Eden sank to grief.
So dawn goes down to day.
Nothing gold can stay.

ROBERT FROST

Now, in groups of three or four, talk about your first impressions. Find out what the others jotted down and what caught their eye.

Then, look at the poem again. You may find it easiest to think of it in two halves.

—In the first four lines the poet is describing something that he has noticed: what?
—In the second half of the poem the poet develops certain thoughts. Can you put them into your own words?

Finally, here is another poem about changing pictures. Share the reading aloud among three voices to bring out the contrasting pictures of the waves breaking on the beach (vss 1 and 4), the hayfield (vss 2 and 5), and the house (vss 3 and 6).

Under the Mountain

Seen from above
The foam in the curving bay is a goose-quill
That feathers . . . unfeathers . . . itself.

Seen from above
The field is a flap and the haycocks buttons
To keep it flush with the earth.

Seen from above
The house is a silent gadget whose purpose
Was long since obsolete.

But when you get down
The breakers are cold scum and the wrack
Sizzles with stinking life.

When you get down
The field is a failed or a worth-while crop, the source
Of back-ache if not heart-ache.

And when you get down
The house is a maelstrom* of loves and hates where you—
Having got down—belong.

* whirlpool

LOUIS MACNEICE

There are several ways of working on this poem. Groups could:
—experiment with different voices for the pairs of verses and rehearse a reading for a live or taped performance. Try reading the verses in blocks of two (vss 1 and 4 etc.) and see whether you prefer this sequence to the poem as printed;
—copy out the poem and illustrate the six verses with miniature drawings alongside the text;
—design a poster which includes the three contrasting scenes, inset with phrases from the poem.

SENSES AND FEELINGS

(i) Five senses

How do you know what's going on around you? Close your eyes for a minute and, without talking to anybody else or touching them, concentrate on what you can hear, touch, smell and taste. Now open your eyes and quickly jot down what you noticed.

If you are sitting in class you can probably *hear* the shuffle of feet, creak and scrape of furniture, whispers and half-stifled giggles around you. Concentrate and try to remember which sounds were close to you (could you hear your own heart?). Which sounds were near? What could you hear in the middle distance? Could you pick up anything from far off?

What could you tell by *touching* things? You may have noticed the cold, hard shape of your pencil, the sharp edge of a piece of paper, the texture of your clothes . . . anything else?

And, resisting the temptation to be rude about your friends, what about *smell*? Polish, leather, plastic, wool, rubber, even cooking smells from the kitchens may all have been noticeable . . . anything else?

Taste probably tells you least of all but there may be something . . . If there is, then jot it down.

Sight, Hearing, Touch, Smell, Taste . . . We rely on our five senses to tell us what's going on. With your eyes closed and without the sense of sight what did you find you were more aware of than you would normally be?

Writers often want their readers to see and feel the same things that they see and feel. They may concentrate hard on what their senses tell them, hoping to recreate the same sort of experience for their reader. This poem is by a writer who is putting off writing: instead she sharpens her pencil. Sight is obviously very important in the poem, but what other senses are brought into play?

Sharpener

The sharpener peels a conical fan,
A paint-trimmed petticoat of scented curls
Tickles my knuckles, rasps spiralling down
And graphite dully shines in finger whorls.

I tap the cold, hard cylinder against my teeth,
Admire its smooth and perfect taper,
Taste damp wood and thin, anaemic lead beneath,
Reluctantly commit myself to paper.

ROSE BENNET

It's an everyday experience closely observed, making us use all our senses. Now try it for yourself, but from memory!

Perhaps you remember going into a science laboratory for the first time.
—What were your first impressions as you entered?
—What sights, sounds and smells hit your senses?
—Can you find words for the taste of some smells?
—Do you remember . . . bottles of chemicals arranged in racks? . . . the cones of flame on the bunsen burners? . . . tall stools and long benches? . . . tripods, flasks and strangely shaped glassware?
—Jot down your ideas quickly and then use them as the basis for a poem which tries to capture the sense of the place as it appeared to you.

Of course you may prefer to choose some other place you know well. What sense impressions would you jot down if you were trying to capture the feeling of being in a gym? on the side of a swimming pool? in the dining hall? . . .

The poet Seamus Heaney likes to make us use all our senses. He was born on a farm in Ireland and many of his poems recall vividly the world of his childhood. If you have ever picked blackberries yourself you will recognise what he describes: if you haven't then the poem may give you a sense of what it is like. As you hear it read ask yourself what senses we need to use in order to share Heaney's experience. Bluebeard, who is mentioned in the poem, by the way, was a murderer.

Blackberry-picking

(for Philip Hobsbaum)

Late August, given heavy rain and sun
For a full week, the blackberries would ripen.
At first, just one, a glossy purple clot
Among others, red, green, hard as a knot.
You ate that first one and its flesh was sweet
Like thickened wine: summer's blood was in it
Leaving stains upon the tongue and lust for
Picking. Then red ones inked up and that hunger
Sent us out with milk-cans, pea-tins, jam-pots
Where briars scratched and wet grass bleached our boots.
We trekked and picked until the cans were full,
Until the tinkling bottom had been covered
With green ones, and on top big dark blobs burned
Like a plate of eyes. Our hands were peppered
With thorn pricks, our palms sticky as Bluebeard's.

We hoarded the fresh berries in the byre.
But when the bath was filled we found a fur,
A rat-grey fungus, glutting on our cache.
The juice was stinking too. Once off the bush
The fruit fermented, the sweet flesh would turn sour.
I always felt like crying. It wasn't fair
That all the lovely canfuls smelt of rot.
Each year I hoped they'd keep, knew they would not.

SEAMUS HEANEY

Quickly, on your own, jot down:

—Any words or phrases that stay in your mind's eye, any pictures that you can *see* clearly.

—Any words or phrases that suggest sounds that you might *hear*.

—Any words or phrases that suggest the *touch* or feel of things.

—Any words or phrases that suggest the *smells* Heaney associates with blackberry-picking.

—Any words or phrases that suggest the *tastes* he remembers from the expedition.

Now, in your groups, compare your ideas and explain why you chose each one.

As well as getting us to use our senses, Seamus Heaney invites us to share his *feelings*. How would you describe his feelings at the beginning of the poem? During the expedition? At the end? How do they change and why do you think they do?

(ii) Feelings

We have seen how Seamus Heaney, by engaging all our senses and persuading us to share his experience, directs us to think about his feelings. Our senses and our feelings are not one and the same, but they may be closely linked. People often say 'whenever I hear that sound . . . smell that smell . . . taste such and such . . . touch this or that—it reminds me of . . . I always think of . . . it makes me feel . . .'

Are there any particular sense impressions that always trigger the same feelings for you? Are there any that make you feel particularly happy? sad? frightened? really set your teeth on edge? . . . Think about this for a moment and then quickly jot down anything that comes to mind. Share your ideas with the group and try to say why things affect you in this way.

Some of the ideas you have shared may be to do with pet hates and fears. D. H. Lawrence writes about a fear that is shared by a lot of people—bats! He feels revulsion and horror seeing them as loathesome creatures.

> Creatures that hang themselves up like an old rag, to sleep;
> And disgustingly upside down.
> Hanging upside down like rows of disgusting old rags
> And grinning in their sleep.
> Bats!

The bats have done him no harm: why do you think he feels like this? Would your feelings be the same if you were in a similar situation? Would something else trigger a similarly violent response in you?

The poet Adrian Henri begins his poem 'Love is . . .' like this:

Love is . . .

Love is feeling cold in the back of vans
Love is a fanclub with only two fans
Love is walking holding paintstained hands
Love is

Each verse of the poem follows the same pattern. Try to write your own poem using the same form perhaps beginning with 'sadness is . . .' or 'fear is . . .'. You could include some of the ideas that have already come up in your discussion. Try, in your own writing, to understand exactly what you feel and why you feel as you do; above all, try to be honest. It's no good writing what you think you ought to feel or what you think your teacher might like you to feel: your poems are you, or they are nothing.

Feeling does not mean wallowing in emotion and it doesn't mean being falsely 'poetic': you know the sort of thing where, for example, all trees become 'majestic', where every daffodil is greeted with rapturous squeals of delight simply because this is thought to be a 'poetic' way of reacting to nature. A poem doesn't convey real feeling if it is only emptiness dressed up in a few fine-sounding words and trimmed with a few 'o'ers' and 'e'ers'. There isn't a special 'soppy' language reserved for use in poems; the best poetry, even when it is about 'traditional' subjects—nature, animals, love, religion, for example—is never soft. Look at D. H. Lawrence's description of unhooking a fish:

Unhooked his gorping, water-horny mouth,
And seen his horror-tiled eye,
His red-gold, water-precious, mirror-flat bright eye;
And felt him beat in my hand, with his mucous, leaping
    life-throb.

There is no slackness here and our senses are alive as we share the vivid experience of seeing and handling the live fish.

William Blake used very simple language when he attacked people's inhuman treatment of animals:

A robin redbreast in a cage
Puts all heaven in a rage.

A horse misused upon the road
Calls to Heaven for human blood.

Each outcry of the hunted hare
A fibre from the brain does tear.

It's very simple, it's direct and it's tough: there is no mistaking the depth of his feelings.

Feelings are often difficult to explain and sometimes unexpected. Why do people enjoy watching a sad play or film or reading a sad book or poem? Why does somebody explain 'I'm crying because I'm so happy'? Are there any villains in films or plays that you 'love to hate'? How is it possible to enjoy being frightened by a horror film? Share your ideas with the group and see how far you agree.

Sometimes, perhaps more often than not, our feelings are complicated—we have 'mixed feelings'—as the writer of the next poem discovered. Listen to it read aloud.

The Lesson

'Your father's gone,' my bald headmaster said.
His shiny dome and brown tobacco jar
Splintered at once in tears. It wasn't grief.
I cried for knowledge which was bitterer
Than any grief. For there and then I knew
That grief has uses—that a father dead
Could bind the bully's fist a week or two;
And then I cried for shame, then for relief.

I was a month past ten when I learnt this:
I still remember how the noise was stilled
In school-assembly when my grief came in.
Some goldfish in a bowl quietly sculled
Around their shining prison on its shelf.
They were indifferent. All the other eyes
Were turned towards me. Somewhere in myself
Pride, like a goldfish, flashed a sudden fin.

EDWARD LUCIE-SMITH

—What does the boy do when he first hears of his father's death?
—Why?
—How do his feelings change?
—Why does he feel pride?

Although these feelings are not perhaps what we might expect a child to feel at the death of a parent, it is clear that this was in fact what happened and that the poet is being quite honest.

Do you always feel as you imagine other people expect you to feel? Have you ever felt guilty that you are not feeling what you are supposed to feel—at the death of a relative perhaps; at succeeding or failing at something; at the way you react to the news of a tragedy or to an Oxfam advertisement . . .? If so, it may be too private to discuss, but you may be able to get your feelings down on paper as a poem.

Roger McGough in this poem explores the feelings of a photographer who accepts commissions to photograph everything from glossy adverts to starving children. At the same time he also invites us to think about our own feelings . . .

Read the first part of the poem below, look at the picture and then turn the page to read the rest of the poem on page 22.

The Commission

In this poem there is a table
Groaning with food.
There is also a child
Groaning for lack of food.
The food is beautifully photographed
The meat more succulent
The fruit as juicy
As you are likely to see.
(The child is sketched in lightly
She is not important.)
The photograph is to be used
In a glossy magazine
As part of a campaign
Advertising after-dinner mints.

This evening the photographer
In receipt of his fee
Celebrates by dining with friends
In a famous West End restaurant.
Doodling on the napkin between courses
The photographer, always creative,
Draws a little Asian girl,
Naked, wide-eyed, pleading.
He has an idea for the next commission.
The one for famine relief.
The tandoori arrives
He puts away his pen
And picks up a fork.

The tone of the poem is deliberately matter-of-fact, almost lacking in feeling you might think at first sight. Is it? What do *you* feel?

IMAGES

(i) Looking and seeing

Some pictures give us the feel of real objects or scenes by selecting and arranging details we can recognise in the world about us. Often it is like looking through a window at something going on outside. Here is an example.

Turn the page and look more closely.

When you look at Constable's *The Cornfield* it's almost as if you can step over the rim and on to the woodland track. Look carefully at this picture. Imagine that you take this step. List what you see and hear in the foreground, middle ground and distance. Compare your jottings with those of your classmates.

Other pictures give us the 'feel' of real objects or scenes by playing down or disguising details we might recognise and concentrating instead on a sense of atmosphere or strong emotion. Here is another example.

In the photograph above the sunlight slants on the sand and the pools but the eye is drawn to the silhouette of the figure and his shadow. What is the atmosphere and what feelings are suggested? Talk in pairs about the picture for a minute or two. It may remind you of places you know.

Poems can make us look both outside and inside ourselves, too. Sometimes the words focus on painting a striking picture to catch the eye. They seem to say 'Stop! Have you noticed this? I like the shape of this tree . . . Look at this chair . . . What a curious face . . .' and so on. The next poem is a clear word-painting built up from details that are easy to recognise.

A Negro Woman

carrying a bunch of marigolds
    wrapped
        in an old newspaper.
She carries them upright,
    bareheaded,
        the bulk
of her thighs
    causing her to waddle
        as she walks
looking into
    the store window which she passes
        on her way.
What is she
    but an ambassador
        from another world
a world of pretty marigolds
    of two shades
        which she announces
not knowing what she does
    other
        than walk the streets
holding the flowers upright
    as a torch
        so early in the morning.

WILLIAM CARLOS WILLIAMS

There she is, a picture caught in words, a simple, bold and colourful
personality.

Other poems avoid the obvious realistic details but, nonetheless, give us a vivid word-picture. For example, how do you write a poem about a rainbow without mentioning any of its colours? Like this!

Rainbow

When you see
de rainbow
you know
God know
wha he doing—
one big smile
across the sky—
I tell you
God got style
the man got style

When you see
raincloud pass
and de rainbow
make a show
I tell you
is God doing
limbo
the man doing
limbo

But sometimes
you know
when I see
de rainbow
so full of glow
and curving
like she bearing child
I does want know
if God
ain't a woman

If that is so
the woman got style
man she got style

JOHN AGARD

The West Indian language and humour give the poem plenty of colour; and there is an unusual idea in the third section. What do you make of it?

Both poems are quite tricky to read aloud. Rehearse readings in pairs or small groups and decide whose voice is best and at what pace the poems should be spoken.

Both poems invite illustration—perhaps a collage of details from colour supplements and magazines for *The Negro Woman*; and maybe a poster that includes the three main shape images of *Rainbow*.

When you have prepared these two, look through the section on word-pictures in the Anthology (pp. 41–66) and select two or three more poems to read aloud which fit in with the idea of 'Images'. You could then present all the poems, live or taped, perhaps introducing each briefly in turn.

(ii) Ideas into pictures

An image is a picture, a way of seeing and a poet is a dealer in images. One technique often used by poets, particularly when they want to express an abstract idea, is that of 'personification'. You will see what this means from these two word-pictures. They were written 400 years ago by Edmund Spenser. Here is his picture of Despair. It's a gloomy portrait to begin with; by the end it is a gory one. Hear the description read aloud, either to the whole class or within a group.

Despair

That darkesome cave they enter, where they find
    That cursed man, low sitting on the ground,
    Musing full sadly in his sullen mind;
    His greasy locks, long growen, and unbound,
    Disordered hung about his shoulders round,
    And hid his face; through which his hollow eyne[1]   [1]eyes
    Looked deadly dull, and stared as astound;
    His raw-bone cheeks through penury and pine,
Were shrunk into his jaws, as he did never dine.

His garment nought but many ragged clouts,
   With thorns together pinned and patched was,
   The which his naked sides he wrapped about;
   And him beside there lay upon the grass
   A dreary corpse, whose life away did pass,
   And wallowed in his own yet lukewarm blood,
   That from his wound still welled fresh alas;
   In which a rusty knife fast fixed stood,
And made an open passage for the gushing flood.

And here is Gluttony. Again, hear the poem read aloud.

Gluttony

And by his side rode loathsome *Gluttony*,
   Deformed creature, on a filthy swine,
   His belly was up-blow with luxury,
   And eke with fatness swollen were his eyne,
   And like a crane his neck was long and fine.
   With which he swallowed up excessive feast,
   For want whereof poor people oft did pine,
   And all the way, most like a brutish beast,
He spewed up his gorge, that all did him deteast.

In green vine leaves he was right fitly clad;
   For other clothes he could not wear for heat,
   And on his head an ivy garland had,
   From under which fast trickled down the sweat:
   Still as he rode, he somewhat still did eat,
   And in his hand did bear a boozing can,
   Of which he supped so oft, that on his seat
   His drunken corpse he scarce upholden can,
In shape and life more like a monster, than a man.

In pairs, talk about the pictures of these two characters that you get in your mind's eye. Then see if you can illustrate these descriptions, perhaps with a poster poem on which you include a few lines as a part of the picture.

Writing about ideas as if they were people is not as difficult as it might seem at first. Some ideas are already associated with well-known personifications—Time as an old man with a scythe; New Year as a baby; or Love as either a mischievous Cupid or a sensuous Venus. In pairs, talk about how you might personify these ideas and others such as Hate, Envy, Anger, Fear, Spring, Winter . . . Is the figure to be male or female? Young or old? What does it look like? What is its mood? List your ideas and then work on *one* of them to make a short description. If you choose Winter then Arcimboldo's painting below may help you with the details.

(iii) Comparisons

Comparison is one of the most common methods used by writers to give us a clear picture of what it is they see and feel. In his poem *Wind* Ted Hughes is constantly comparing things. Read it aloud.

> This house has been far out at sea all night,
> The woods crashing through darkness, the booming hills,
> Winds stampeding the fields under the window
> Floundering black astride and blinding wet
>
> Till day rose; then under an orange sky
> The hills had new places, and wind wielded
> Blade-light, luminous black and emerald,
> Flexing like the lens of a mad eye.
>
> At noon I scaled along the house-side as far as
> The coal-house door. I dared once to look up—
> Through the brunt wind that dented the balls of my eyes
> The tent of the hills drummed and strained its guyrope,
>
> The fields quivering, the skyline a grimace,
> At any second to bang and vanish with a flap:
> The wind flung a magpie away and a black-
> Back gull bent like an iron bar slowly. The house
>
> Rang like some fine green goblet in the note
> That any second would shatter it. Now deep
> In chairs, in front of the great fire, we grip
> Our hearts and cannot entertain book, thought,
>
> Or each other. We watch the fire blazing,
> And feel the roots of the house move, but sit on,
> Seeing the window tremble to come in,
> Hearing the stones cry out under the horizons.

Before you talk about the poem, re-read it to yourself and spend five or ten minutes making your own notes. Jottings *around* the poem about things you notice are often a good way-in. You could either write out the text yourself (this is a useful way of attending to the words carefully), or use a separate copy. Your notes might look something like this:

house like a ship in a storm

, This house has been far out at sea all night

lots of
active verbs
suggest
galeforce winds

The woods crashing Through darkness, the booming hills — sounds
Winds stampeding the fields under the window
Floundering black astride and blinding wet

These are two or three things we noticed about the first verse. Continue with your own notes for the rest of the poem. Some of Hughes' images in this poem are unusual and perhaps puzzling. When you have made your own jottings, spend some time in a group finding out what each of you has noticed about the poem. In particular, which comparisons seemed most vivid? One of them may suggest an idea for an illustration to accompany a phrase or line from the poem; or, as a group, you could divide up the verses and work on a picture sequence for the whole text. Notice how the poem moves from darkness to dawn, to noon, to afternoon, and finishes, it seems, in front of the evening fire.

As you talked about the poem *Wind* you probably noticed how the same images meant different things to different people. In each of the following extracts the writer has captured his subject in an original way by using comparisons. Read them through to yourself, and choose two or three which you like for whatever reasons. Make a note of *what* you like in the lines you have chosen. (It may be useful to copy out your choices and add your jottings, as you did before.)

(1) *A moose*

The goofy Moose, the walking house-frame,
Is lost
In the forest. He bumps, he blunders, he stands.

With massy bony thoughts sticking out near his ears—
Reaching out palm upwards, to catch whatever might be falling
    from heaven—
He tries to think,
Leaning their huge weight
On the lectern of his front legs.

TED HUGHES

32

(2) *A pineapple*
   The hut stands by itself beneath the palms.
   Out of their bottle the green genii come.
   A vine has climbed the other side of the wall.

   The sea is spouting upward out of rocks. . . .

   The lozenges are nailed-up lattices.
   The owl sits humped. It has a hundred eyes.
   The cocoanut and cockerel in one.

WALLACE STEVENS

(3) *A waterfall*
   It appears an athletic glacier
   Has reared into reverse: is swallowed up
   And regurgitated through this long throat.

SEAMUS HEANEY

(4) *A docker*
   There, in the corner, staring at his drink.
   The cap juts like a gantry's crossbeam,
   Cowling plated forehead and sledgehead jaw.
   Speech is clamped in the lips' vice.

SEAMUS HEANEY

(5) *A kangaroo*
   Her little loose hands, and drooping Victorian shoulders,
   And then her great weight below the waist, her vast
      pale belly
   With a thin young yellow little paw hanging out, and
      straggle of a long thin ear, like ribbon,
   Like a funny trimming to the middle of her belly, thin
      little dangle of an immature paw, and one thin ear.

D. H. LAWRENCE

(6) *The imprint of a sea-shell on a stone*
   And chiselled clear on stone
   A spider-web of shell,
   The thumb-print of the sea.

N. NICHOLSON

(7) A stagnant pond in a city
    Daily it sweltered in the punishing sun.
    Bubbles gargled delicately, bluebottles
    Wove a strong gauze of sound around the smell.

SEAMUS HEANEY

(8) Fog
    The yellow fog that rubs its back upon the window-panes,
    The yellow smoke that rubs its muzzle on the window-panes
    Licked its tongue into the corners of the evening,
    Lingered upon the pools that stand in drains,
    Let fall upon its back the soot that falls from chimneys,
    Slipped by the terrace, made a sudden leap,
    And seeing that it was a soft October night,
    Curled once about the house, and fell asleep.

T. S. ELIOT

(9) Thistle
    Thistle, blue bunch of daggers
    rattling upon the wind,
    saw-tooth that separates
    the lips of grasses.

LAURIE LEE

(10) Pigeons
    Small blue busybodies
    Strutting like fat gentlemen
    With hands clasped
    Under their swallowtail coats

RICHARD KELL

(11) Ice

        Ice
Has got its spearhead into place.

First a skin, delicately here
Restraining a ripple from the air;

Soon plate and rivet on pond and brook;
Then tons of chain and massive lock

To hold rivers . . .

TED HUGHES

(12) A schoolboy

Timothy Winters comes to school
With eyes as wide as a football-pool,
Ears like bombs and teeth like splinters:
A blitz of a boy is Timothy Winters.

CHARLES CAUSLEY

(13) Storm in the Black Forest

Now it is almost night, from the bronzey soft sky
jugfall after jugfull of pure white liquid fire, bright white
tipples over and spills down,
and is gone
and gold-bronze flutters bent through the thick upper air.

And as the electric liquid pours out, sometimes
a still brighter white snake wriggles among it, spilled
and tumbling wriggling down the sky . . .

D. H. LAWRENCE

When you have made your own choices, discuss in groups which
images you prefer. Are there any that you do not *see* at all? *Does* the
same image mean different things to different people?

Now, as a group task, try inventing some images of your own.
Choose your own subject, one that you could describe in several
ways (your desk lid, electricity pylons, the London Underground, a
tower block, say) and each of you make up one line or phrase, using
a comparison if possible, to describe it. Sort out the best order for
your lines, think of a title, and write out your group poem.

(iv) Developing images

In the next poem the writer has created several images—just as you have been attempting to do—each of which helps the reader to see more clearly what is being described. Hear the poem read aloud.

Cow in Calf

It seems she has swallowed a barrel.
From forelegs to haunches
her belly is slung like a hammock.

Slapping her out of the byre is like slapping
a great bag of seed. My hand
tingled as if strapped, but I had to
hit her again and again and
heard the blows plump like a depth-charge
far in her gut.

The udder grows. Windbags
of bagpipes are crammed there
to drone in her lowing.
Her cud and her milk, her heats and her calves
keep coming and going.

SEAMUS HEANEY

Again, spend five minutes re-reading and jotting down two or three phrases or lines which give you a picture in your mind's eye.

All the comparisons in the poem, although very different from each other, are used to capture one particular quality of the cow in calf. Talk in pairs and try to put this overall impression into your own words.

So far you have read and written images which are brief—probably of no more than two or three lines. The poem which follows combines many of the qualities discussed in earlier sections—pictures of things seen and heard, pictures of feelings and ideas, sense impressions, personifications—as well as sustaining a comparison all the way through the poem. First, read the poem through to yourself.

The Rooster

1 Why is it
  The roustabout Rooster, raging at the dawn
  Wakes us so early?

2 A warrior-king is on fire!
  His armour is all crooked daggers and scimitars
  And it's shivering red-hot—with rage!

  And he screams out through his megaphone:
3 'Give me back my Queens!'

1 What's happened?

  He fell asleep, a King of Tropic India
  With ten thousand concubines, each one
  Gorgeous as a volcanic sunset—

2 But now he wakes, turned inside out—a rooster!
  With eleven flea-bitten hens!

  And he remembers it all. No wonder he screeches:
3 'Give me back my Queens!'

2 No wonder his scarlet cheeks vibrate like a trumpet!

1 But it's no use. He seems to droop.
  It's simply no use.
  All that majestic armour is just feathers.

2 But now it comes over him again!
  Again he goes all stiff—and quivering!
  He aims himself at the sun.
  He looks like a flame-thrower,
  And with one blast, as if it were his last,
  Tries to turn himself back outside in
3 With: 'Give me back my Queens!'

1 The sun yawns and saunters away among some clouds.
  The empty-headed hens
  Are happy unriddling the cinders.

  Only the cockerel dreams and trembles and flames.

TED HUGHES

In groups of three rehearse a reading of the poem. The numbers down the side of the text show where each reader takes over. You will soon see that 1 is the narrator, 2 is a more urgent voice building up to the climax each time, and 3 is the shriek of the cock-crow. You could perform your readings live, or perhaps tape-record them.

As you are preparing your version, ask yourselves: What is the main image of the rooster that recurs through the poem? What is the difference between his dream-picture of himself and his actual life among the hens?

PART B

Anthology

WORD-PICTURES

The Poor Man's Son

Poverty's child—
he starts to grind the rice,
and gazes at the moon,

BASHO

The Weeping Willow

How strong a green
are the strings of willow branches:
the flowing of the stream!

ONITSURA

A Wish

I'd like enough drinks
to put me to sleep—on stones
covered with pinks.

BASHO

The Cuckoo's Song

As the cuckoo flies,
its singing stretches out:
upon the water lies.

BASHO

City People

Townsfolk, it is plain—
carrying red maple leaves
in the homebound train.

MEISETSU

Kitten in a tree

He sat,
a small ball of spikes
stuck in a tree,
fierce as a miniature medieval-club;
a pom-pom of thorns.

We brought him down
and plump with milk,
he is a singing powder-puff
vibrating silk.

ISOBEL THRILLING

Light Poem

Our street lights are all provided
with little shelters, like mexican hats,
wide-brimmed over their long faces.

Late at night they beam proudly from beneath
their brims, vying with each other
and the moon's shed silk. Yet earlier,

if you are quick, see their reserved glow,
blushingly embarrassed to be caught
always hanging about on street corners.

MARTYN CRUCEFIX

Springtime Rain

Springtime rain: together,
Intent upon their talking, go
Straw-raincoat and umbrella.

BUSON

The Red Cockatoo

Sent as a present from Annam—
A red cockatoo.
Coloured like the peach-tree blossom,
Speaking with the speech of men.
And they did to it what is always done
To the learned and eloquent.
They took a cage with stout bars
And shut it up inside.

PO CHU-I
(*Trans. Arthur Waley*)

Cock-Crow

Out of the wood of thoughts that grows by night
To be cut down by the sharp axe of light,—
Out of the night, two cocks together crow,
Cleaving the darkness with a silver blow:
And bright before my eyes twin trumpeters stand,
Heralds of splendour, one at either hand,
Each facing each as in a coat of arms:
The milkers lace their boots up at the farms.

EDWARD THOMAS

Fan-Piece, for her Imperial Lord

O fan of white silk,
   clear as frost on the grass-blade,
You also are laid aside.

EZRA POUND

Fallen Flower

Fallen flower I see
Returning to its branch—
Ah! a butterfly.

A. MORITAKE
(*Trans. G. Bownas and A. Thwaite*)

The Falling Flower

In the lamplight's vermilion shade
The dark red peony unfolds
Its hundred-petalled fans.
The fire's coral breath unloads
In a random shower
This quietly exploding rose.

Slowly the stillness
Lets handfuls of petals fall.
On the pink-checked tablecloth
Softly the flower pounces,
Weighing this dying hour
In its own crimson ounces.

JAMES KIRKUP

Flower Dump

Cannas shiny as slag,
Slug-soft stems,
Whole beds of bloom pitched on a pile,
Carnations, verbenas, cosmos,
Moulds, weeds, dead leaves,
Turned-over roots
With bleached veins
Twined like fine hair,
Each clump in the shape of a pot;
Everything limp
But one tulip on top,
One swaggering head
Over the dying, the newly dead.

THEODORE ROETHKE

To Paint a Water Lily

A green level of lily leaves
Roofs the pond's chamber and paves

The flies' furious arena: study
These, the two minds of this lady.

First observe the air's dragonfly
That eats meat, that bullets by

Or stands in space to take aim;
Others as dangerous comb the hum

Under the trees. There are battle-shouts
And death-cries everywhere hereabouts

But inaudible, so the eyes praise
To see the colours of these flies

Rainbow their arcs, spark, or settle
Cooling like beads of molten metal

Through the spectrum. Think what worse
Is the pond-bed's matter of course;

Prehistoric bedragonned times
Crawl that darkness with Latin names,

Have evolved no improvements there,
Jaws for heads, the set stare,

Ignorant of age as of hour—
Now paint the long-necked lily-flower

Which, deep in both worlds, can be still
As a painting, trembling hardly at all

Though the dragonfly alight,
Whatever horror nudge her root.

TED HUGHES

To Paint the Portrait of a Bird

To Elsa Henriquez

First paint a cage
with an open door
then paint
something pretty
something simple
something beautiful
something useful . . .
for the bird
then place the canvas against a tree
in a garden
in a wood
or in a forest
hide behind the tree
without speaking
without moving . . .
Sometimes the bird comes quickly
but he can just as well spend long years
before deciding
Don't get discouraged
wait
wait years if necessary
the swiftness or slowness of the coming
of the bird having no rapport
with the success of the picture
When the bird comes
if he comes
observe the most profound silence
wait till the bird enters the cage
and when he has entered
gently close the door with a brush
then
paint out all the bars one by one
taking care not to touch any of the feathers of the bird
Then paint the portrait of the tree
choosing the most beautiful of its branches

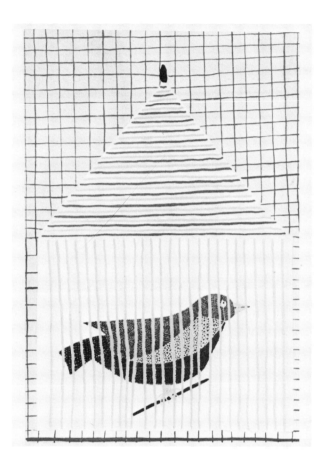

for the bird
paint also the green foliage and the wind's freshness
the dust of the sun
and the noise of the insects in the summer heat
and then wait for the bird to decide to sing
If the bird doesn't sing
it's a bad sign
a sign that the painting is bad
but if he sings it's a good sign
a sign that you can sign
So then so very gently you pull out
one of the feathers of the bird
and you write your name in the corner of the picture.

JACQUES PREVERT
(*Trans. Lawrence Ferlinghetti*)

A Game

They are throwing the ball
To and fro between them,
In and out of the picture.
She is in the painting
Hung on the wall
In a narrow gold frame.
He stands on the floor
Catching and tossing
At the right distance.
She wears a white dress,
Black boots and stockings,
And a flowered straw hat.
She moves in silence
But it seems from her face
That she must be laughing.
Behind her is sunlight
And a tree-filled garden;
You might think to hear
Birds or running water,
But no, there is nothing.
Once or twice he has spoken
But does so no more,
For she cannot answer.
So he stands smiling,
Playing her game
(She is almost a child),
Not daring to go,
Intent on the ball.
And she is the same.
For what would result
Neither wishes to know
If it should fall.

FLEUR ADCOCK

The Optimist

The optimist builds himself safe inside a cell
and paints the inside walls sky-blue
and blocks up the door
and says he's in heaven.

D. H. LAWRENCE

From a Boat at Coniston

I look into the lake (the lacquered water
Black with the sunset), watching my own face.
Tiny red-ribbed fishes swim
In and out of the nostrils, long-tongued weeds
Lick at the light that oozes down from the surface,
And bubbles rise from the eyes like aerated
Tears shed there in the element of mirrors.
My sight lengthens its focus; sees the sky
Laid level upon the glass, the loud
World of the wind and the map-making clouds and history
Squinting over the rim of the fell. The wind
Lets on the water, paddling like a duck,
And face and cloud are grimaced out
In inch-deep wrinkles of the moving waves.
A blackbird clatters; alder leaves
Make mooring buoys for the water beetles.
I wait for the wind to drop, against hope
Hoping, and against the weather, yet to see
The water empty, the water full of itself,
Free of the sky and the cloud and free of me.

NORMAN NICHOLSON

Corner Seat

Suspended in a moving night
The face in the reflected train
Looks at first sight as self-assured
As your own face—But look again:
Windows between you and the world
Keep out the cold, keep out the fright;
Then why does your reflection seem
So lonely in the moving night?

LOUIS MACNEICE

The Round Pond

Ducks squat at the edge of clouds.
Kites glide stealthily like pikes.
A white yacht makes a voyage
To nowhere. Two small boys
Poke sticks into their jelly likenesses.
Parents, dogs, foreigners, predatory
Girls stand round the pond
Like minutes on a clock.

VICKI FEAVER

Water Picture

In the pond in the park
all things are doubled:
Long buildings hang and
wriggle gently. Chimneys
are bent legs bouncing
on clouds below. A flag
wags like a fishhook
down there in the sky.

The arched stone bridge
is an eye, with underlid
in the water. In its lens
dip crinkled heads with hats
that don't fall off. Dogs go by,
barking on their backs.
A baby, taken to feed the
ducks, dangles upside-down,
a pink balloon for a buoy.

Treetops deploy a haze of
cherry bloom for roots,
where birds coast belly-up
in the glass bowl of a hill;
from its bottom a bunch
of peanut-munching children
is suspended by their
sneakers, waveringly.

A swan, with twin necks
forming the figure three,
steers between two dimpled
towers doubled. Fondly
hissing, she kisses herself,
and all the scene is troubled:
water-windows splinter,
tree-limbs tangle, the bridge
folds like a fan.

MAY SWENSON

Reflections

The mirror above my fireplace reflects the reflected
Room in my windows; I look in the mirror at night
And see two rooms, the first where left is right
And the second, beyond the reflected window, corrected
But there I am standing back to my back. The standard
Lamp comes thrice in my mirror, twice in my window,
The fire in the mirror lies two rooms away through the
   window,

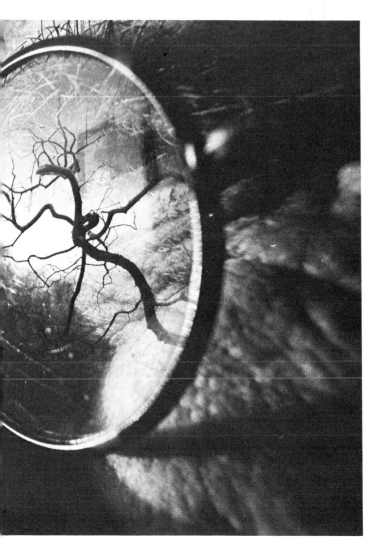

The fire in the window lies one room away down the terrace,
My actual room stands sandwiched between confections
Of night and lights and glass and in both directions
I can see beyond and through the reflections the street lamps
At home outdoors where my indoors rooms lie stranded,
Where a taxi perhaps will drive in through the bookcase
Whose books are not for reading and past the fire
Which gives no warmth and pull up by my desk
At which I cannot write since I am not lefthanded.

LOUIS MACNEICE

Mushrooms

Overnight, very
Whitely, discreetly,
Very quietly

Our toes, our noses
Take hold on the loam,
Acquire the air.

Nobody sees us,
Stops us, betrays us;
The small grains make room.

Soft fists insist on
Heaving the needles,
The leafy bedding,

Even the paving.
Our hammers, our rams,
Earless and eyeless,

Perfectly voiceless,
Widen the crannies,
Shoulder through holes. We

Diet on water,
On crumbs of shadow,
Bland-mannered, asking

Little or nothing.
So many of us!
So many of us!

We are shelves, we are
Tables, we are meek,
We are edible,

Nudgers and shovers
In spite of ourselves.
Our kind multiplies:

We shall by morning
Inherit the earth.
Our foot's in the door.

SYLVIA PLATH

60

Full Moon and Little Frieda

A cool small evening shrunk to a dog bark and the clank
   of a bucket—

And you listening.
A spider's web, tense for the dew's touch.
A pail lifted, still and brimming—mirror
To tempt a first star to a tremor.

Cows are going home in the lane there, looping the
   hedges with their warm wreaths of breath—
A dark river of blood, many boulders,
Balancing unspilled milk.

'Moon!' you cry suddenly, 'Moon! Moon!'

The moon has stepped back like an artist gazing amazed
   at a work
That points at him amazed.

TED HUGHES

Child Waiting

(for lesley)

little head
at the window
in childeyed wonder

the ceaseless
come and go
of mighty traffic
must be moving magic
to your unblinking gaze

but how patient
are eyes looking for one
named mummy
in a rumble of wheels

JOHN AGARD

The Motion of the Earth

A day with sky so wide,
So stripped of cloud, so scrubbed, so vacuumed free
Of dust, that you can see
The earth-line as a curve, can watch the blue
Wrap over the edge, looping round and under,
Making you wonder
Whether the dark has anywhere left to hide.
But the world is slipping away; the polished sky
Gives nothing to grip on; clicked from the knuckle
The marble rolls along the gutter of time—
Earth, star and galaxy
Shifting their place in space.
Noon, sunset, clouds, the equably varying weather,
The diffused light, the illusion of blue,
Conceal each hour a different constellation.
All things are new
Over the sun, but we,
Our eyes on our shoes, go staring
At the asphalt, the gravel, the grass at the roadside, the
    door-
step, the doodles of snails, the crochet of mortar and lime,
Seeking the seeming familiar, though every stride
Takes us a thousand miles from where we were before.

NORMAN NICHOLSON

529 1983

Absentmindedly,
sometimes,
I lift the receiver
And dial my own number.

What revelations,
I think then,
if only
I could get through to myself.

GERDA MAYER

In The Microscope

Here too are dreaming landscapes,
lunar, derelict.
Here too are the masses
tillers of the soil.
And cells, fighters
who lay down their lives
for a song.

Here too are cemeteries,
fame and snow.
And I hear murmuring,
the revolt of immense estates.

MIROSLAV HOLUB
(*Trans. I. Milner and G. Theiner*)

Film Put in Backwards

When I woke
I woke in the breathless black
Of the box.
        I heard: the earth
Was opening over me. Clods
Fluttered back
        To the shovel. The
Dear box, with me the dear
        Departed, gently rose.
The lid flew up and I
Stood feeling:
        Three bullets travel
Out of my chest
Into rifles of soldiers, who
        Marched off, gasping
Out of the air a song
With calm firm steps
        Backwards.

GÜNTER KUNERT

Haiku. Remind yourself of the 5–7–5 haiku syllable pattern (p. 8). Think about this advice from one of Japan's greatest haiku poets, Shiki:

> Remember perspective. Large things are large, but small things are also large if seen close up . . .
> Keep the words tight; put in nothing useless.
> Cut down as much as possible on adverbs and verbs.
> Use both imaginary pictures and real ones, but prefer the real ones.

(from *An Introduction to Haiku* by H. G. Henderson, Doubleday Anchor, p. 161)

In pairs, note down and talk about a few things which you have studied closely—a leaf? an insect? a stamp?—perhaps with the aid of a magnifying glass. Discuss the details and jot down any words or phrases or comparisons that come to mind. Then, each of you choose *one* of the objects from your list and, when writing your haiku about it, try to take Shiki's advice.

Sequel. Re-read D. H. Lawrence's poem *The Optimist* (p. 53). What might a pessimist do? Invent a similar poem as an answer.

Definitions
Our ideas about big, complicated issues can often be defined quite sharply in terms of word-pictures.
Boys of your own age defined Death as
  'beyond the night without your father'
and Fear as
  'a very dark room with very white curtains'.
Perhaps you could attempt your own definitions of some of the following: Time, Beginning, Insincerity, Evil, Fear, Death, Hunger, Love, Loneliness, Wisdom, Happiness.

Performance. In Sylvia Plath's *Mushrooms* (p. 60) non-human things seem to have a life of their own. Prepare a reading of the poem so that you can perform it, either live or taped. Rehearse it in fairly large groups, giving out the phrases among different voices, perhaps combining on the lines 'So many of us!/So many of us!' and again at the end.

  —In groups, prepare a reading of *To Paint the Portrait of a Bird* (p. 50). You will need to work out where the best 'hand-over' places come; they seem to occur every four to eight lines.

Reflections. On pages 53–59 there are several poems and pictures about reflections in lakes, ponds, windows and mirrors. In pairs, talk about what you read and see.

—Which poem gives you the best reflection?

—Do any of the poems or pictures remind you of reflections you often see?

Choose one example you know well and, by yourself, list all the things you notice about this reflection. For instance, reflections in water often produce strange effects because things seen at different levels merge into each other. If you imagine looking down from a bridge into slow-moving water you might list objects on the surface—floating litter, water-flies, oil slicks; then perhaps, the reflections of yourself and your surroundings. Next, you may pick out sediment, weed, perhaps fish—things moving in the water; and, at the deepest level, perhaps you can make out the stones, tin-cans and other debris on the bottom. Write up your list into a descriptive poem. Illustrate it if you can.

Poems and pictures. *Water-picture* (p. 56) and *A Round Pond* (p. 54) lend themselves to illustration—perhaps a poster poem?

—Read through *A Game* (p. 52) and talk about what is happening in the poem. Could you write about a favourite picture in the same way?

PEOPLE

Waiting for Thelma's Laughter

(for Thelma, my West Indian born Afro-American neighbour)

You wanna take the world
in hand
and fix-it-up
the way you fix your living room

You wanna reach out and crush
life's big and small injustices
in the fire and honey
of your hands

You wanna scream
cause your head's too small
for your dreams

and the children
                running round
                    acting like lil clowns
                        breaking the furniture down

while I sit through
it all watching you
knowing any time now
your laughter's gonna come

to drown and heal us all

                                        GRACE NICHOLS

I love me mudder (mother) . . .

I love me mudder and me mudder love me
we come so far from over de sea,
we heard dat de streets were paved with gold
sometime it hot sometime it cold
I love me mudder and me mudder love me
we try fe live in harmony
you might know her as Valerie
but to me she is my mummy.

She shouts at me daddy so loud some time
she don't smoke weed she don't drink wine
she always do the best she can
she work damn hard down ina England,
she's always singing some kind of song
she have big muscles and she very very strong,
she likes pussy cats and she love cashew nuts
she don't bother with no if and buts.

I love me mudder and me mudder love me
we come so far from over de sea
we heard dat de streets were paved with gold
sometime it hot sometime it cold,
I love her and she love me too
and dis is a love I know is true
my family unit extends to you
loving each other is de ting to do.

BENJAMIN ZEPHANIAH

The lament of the banana man

Gal, I'm tellin' you, I'm tired fo' true,
Tired of Englan', tired o' you.
But I can' go back to Jamaica now . . .

I'm here in Englan', I'm drawin' pay,
I go to de underground every day—
Eight hours is all, half-hour fo' lunch,
M' uniform's free, an' m' ticket punch—
Punchin' tickets not hard to do,
When I'm tired o' punching', I let dem through.

I get a paid holiday once a year.
Ol' age an' sickness can' touch me here.

I have a room o' m' own, an' a iron bed,
Dunlopillo under m' head,
A Morphy-Richards to warm de air,
A formica table, an easy chair.
I have summer clothes, an' winter clothes,
An' paper kerchiefs to blow m' nose.

My yoke is easy, my burden is light,
I know a place I can go to, any night.
Dis place Englan'! I'm not complainin',
If it col', it col', if it rainin', it rainin'.
I don' min' if it's mostly night,
Dere's always inside, or de sodium light.

I don' min' white people starin' at me
Dey don' want me here? Don't is deir country?
You won' catch me bawlin' any homesick tears
If I don' see Jamaica fo' a t'ousan' years!

. . . Gal, I'm tellin' you, I'm tired fo' true,
Tired of Englan', tired o' you,
I can't go back to Jamaica now—
But I'd want to die there, anyhow.

EVAN JONES

Listn Big Brodda Dread, Na!

My sista is younga dan mi.
My sista outsmart five-foot three.
My sista is own car repairer
and yu nah catch me doin judo with her.

> I sey I wohn get a complex.
> I wohn get a complex.
> Den I see de muscles my sista flex.

My sista is tops at disco dance.
My sista is well into self-reliance.
My sista plays guitar and drums
and wahn si her knock back double rums.

> I sey I wohn get a complex.
> I wohn get a complex.
> Den I see de muscles my sista flex.

My sista doesn mind smears of grease and dirt.
My sista'll reduce you with sheer muscle hurt.
My sista says no guy goin keep her phone-bound—
wid own car mi sista is a wheel-hound.

> I sey I wohn get a complex.
> I wohn get a complex.
> Den I see de muscles my sista flex.

JAMES BERRY

Poem For My Sister

My little sister likes to try my shoes,
to strut in them,
admire her spindle-thin twelve-year-old legs
in this season's styles.
She says they fit her perfectly,
but wobbles
on their high heels, they're
hard to balance.

I like to watch my little sister
playing hopscotch, admire the neat hops-and-skips of her,
their quick peck,
never-missing their mark, not
over-stepping the line.
She is competent at peever.

I try to warn my little sister
about unsuitable shoes,
point out my own distorted feet, the callouses,
odd patches of hard skin.
I should not like to see her
in my shoes.
I wish she should stay
sure footed,
          sensibly shod.

LIZ LOCHHEAD

Advice to a teenage daughter

You have found a new war-game
called Love.
Here on your dressing-table
stand arrayed
brave ranks of lipsticks
brandishing
swords of cherry pink and flame.
Behold the miniature armies
of little jars,
packed with the scented
dynamite of flowers.
See the dreaded tweezers;
tiny pots
of manufactured moonlight,
stick-on-stars.

Beware my sweet;
conquest may seem easy
but you can't compete with football,
motor-cycles, cars,
cricket, computer-games,
or a plate of chips.

ISOBEL THRILLING

Street Boy

Just you look at me, man,
Stompin' down the street
My crombie stuffed with biceps
My boots is filled with feet.

Just you hark to me, man,
When they call us out
My head is full of silence
My mouth is full of shout.

Just you watch me move, man,
Steady like a clock
My heart is spaced on blue beat
My soul is stoned on rock.

Just you read my name, man,
Writ for all to see
The walls is red with stories
The streets is filled with me.

GARETH OWEN

Out and About, the Lads

pants flapping round legpoles
like denim flags

necks open to the wind
their element

boots the colour of raw liver
boss the pavement

out and about
the lads

voices raised like fists
tattooed with curses

outnumbered rivals
they take in their stride

lampposts and pillarboxes
step aside

out and about
the lads

thick as thieves
and every one a star

Paul uses a knife
you dont feel a thing

Des the best speller
the aerosol king

out and about
the lads

cornered young
they will live their lives in corners

umpteenagers
out on a spree

looking for the likes
of you and me

out and about
the lads.

ROGER McGOUGH

The Ballad of Charlotte Dymond

It was a Sunday evening
And in the April rain
That Charlotte went from our house
And never came home again.

Her shawl of diamond redcloth
She wore a yellow gown,
She carried the green gauze handkerchief
She bought in Bodmin town.

About her throat her necklace
And in her purse her pay:
The four silver shillings
She had at Lady Day.

In her purse four shillings
And in her purse her pride.
As she walked out one evening
Her lover at her side.

Out beyond the marshes
Where the cattle stand,
With her crippled lover
Limping at her hand.

Charlotte walked with Matthew
Through the Sunday mist,
Never saw the razor
Waiting at his wrist.

Charlotte she was gentle
But they found her in the flood
Her Sunday beads among the reeds
Beaming with her blood.

Matthew, where is Charlotte,
And wherefore has she flown?
For you walked out together
And now are come alone.

Why do you not answer,
Stand silent as a tree,
Your Sunday worsted stockings
All muddied to the knee?

Why do you mend your breast-pleat
With a rusty needle's thread
And fall with fears and silent tears
Upon your single bed?

Why do you sit so sadly
Your face the colour of clay
And with a green gauze handkerchief
Wipe the sour sweat away?

Has she gone to Blisland
To seek an easier place?
And is that why your eye won't dry
And blinds your bleaching face?

'Take me home!' cried Charlotte,
'I lie here in the pit!'
A red rock rests upon my breasts
And my naked neck is split!'

Her skin was soft as sable,
Her eyes were wide as day,
Her hair was blacker than the bog
That licked her life away.

Her cheeks were made of honey,
Her throat was made of flame
Where all around the razor
Had written its red name.

As Matthew turned at Plymouth
About the tilting Hoe,
The cold and cunning Constable
Up to him did go.

'I've come to take you, Matthew,
Unto the Magistrate's door.
Come quiet now, you pretty poor boy,
And you must know what for.'

'She is as pure,' cried Matthew,
'As is the early dew,
Her only stain it is the pain
That round her neck I drew!

'She is as guiltless as the day
She sprang forth from her mother.
The only sin upon her skin
Is that she loved another.'

They took him off to Bodmin,
They pulled the prison bell,
They sent him smartly up to heaven
And dropped him down to Hell.

All through the granite kingdom
And on its travelling airs
Ask which of these two lovers
The most deserves your prayers.

And your steel heart search, Stranger
That you may pause and pray
For lovers who come not to bed
Upon their wedding day.

But lie upon the moorland
Where stands the sacred snow
Above the breathing river,
And the salt sea-winds go.

CHARLES CAUSLEY

A Poison Tree

I was angry with my friend:
I told my wrath, my wrath did end.
I was angry with my foe:
I told it not, my wrath did grow.

And I water'd it in fears,
Night and morning with my tears;
And I sunnéd it with smiles,
And with soft deceitful wiles.

And it grew both day and night,
Till it bore an apple bright;
And my foe beheld it shine,
And he knew that it was mine,

And into my garden stole
When the night had veil'd the pole:
In the morning glad I see
My foe outstretch'd beneath the tree.

WILLIAM BLAKE

Five Epitaphs

Facts of Death

The play is over:
You can die now.

G. P. WALLEY

Charles the Second

Here lies our Sovereign Lord the King,
    Whose word no man relies on,
Who never said a foolish thing,
    Nor ever did a wise one.

JOHN WILMOT

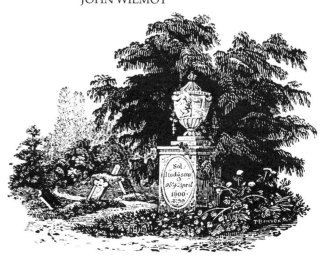

On a Pessimist

I'm Smith of Stoke, aged sixty-odd,
  I've lived without a dame
From youth-time on; and would to God
  My dad had done the same.

THOMAS HARDY
(from the French and Greek)

Matthew Bird

I, the Reverend Matthew Bird,
Preacher of God's Holy Word,
Taking leave of aisle and pew,
Go to find how much is true.

L. A. G. STRONG

Lather As You Go

Beneath this slab
John Brown is stowed.
He watched the ads,
And not the road.

Ogden Nash

Performing. One of the most exciting developments in poetry in recent years has been the much wider publication of poems by black writers from Africa and the Caribbean. This section on 'People' begins with four poems by black writers each of which paints a vivid picture of a single character. In groups, try one or two of the poems over, reading them aloud and getting a feel for the language and the rhythms. When you feel fairly confident, try to turn your reading into a performance for the group or the whole class. You could choose to make a tape-recording linking all four poems together.

Talking and writing. Maybe you recognise the picture Isobel Thrilling paints when she offers advice to her teenage daughter on page 73. Is it sound advice? What might a matching poem giving Advice to a Teenager's Parents or Advice to a Teenage Son be like?

Performing. The poems on pages 74 and 76, *Street Boy* and *Out And About, the Lads* show teenage boys acting tough. Both poems can be performed. *Street Boy* goes well with four different voices, one for each verse. *Out And About, the Lads* could be performed using a different voice for each pair of lines followed by the whole group saying 'Out and about, the Lads' in different tones—tough, exuberant, menacing . . . Do the writers get it right? Is this how teenage boys are?

Performing and Writing. Charlotte Dymond was a young Cornish girl who was tragically murdered by her lover, Matthew, because he believed she loved another. Charles Causley has used the old ballad form in his poem on page 77 to retell her story. Listen to the poem being read through once and then, in groups, divide up the poem and produce your own reading of it with different voices taking different parts.

You might like to tackle writing your own ballad: it isn't as difficult as it might seem. Take a story from the newspaper and try to tell it simply in verses of four lines each. Aim to make the last words of the second and fourth lines rhyme in each verse.

Epitaphs. On pages 81 to 83 you will find a number of epitaphs. Try to write one or two of your own and present them as though carved on a tombstone.

PLACES

Island Man

(for a Caribbean island man in London who still wakes up to the sound of the sea)

Morning
and island man wakes up
to the sound of blue surf
in his head
the steady breaking and wombing

wild seabirds
and fishermen pushing out to sea
the sun surfacing defiantly

from the east
of his small emerald island
he always comes back   groggily groggily

Comes back to sands
of a grey metallic soar
                          to surge of wheels
to dull North Circular roar

muffling muffling
his crumpled pillow waves
island man heaves himself

Another London day

GRACE NICHOLS

Shantytown

High on the veld upon that plain
And far from streets and lights and cars
And bare of trees, and bare of grass,
Jabavu* sleeps beneath the stars.   * Shantytown area near Johannesburg.

Jabavu sleeps.
The children cough.
Cold creeps up, the hard night cold,
The earth is tight within its grasp,
The highveld cold without soft rain,
Dry as the sand, rough as a rasp.

The frost rimmed night invades the shacks.
Through dusty ground
Through rocky ground
Through freezing ground the night cold creeps
In cotton blankets, rags and sacks
Beneath the stars Jabavu sleeps.

One day Jabavu will awake
To greet a new and shining day.
The sound of coughing will become
The children's laughter as they play
In parks with flowers where dust now swirls
In strong-walled homes with warmth and light.
But for tonight Jabavu sleeps
Jabavu sleeps. The stars are bright.

ANON (*South Africa*)

Earthquake

An old man's flamingo-coloured kite
Twitches higher over tiled roofs.
Idly gazing through the metal gauze
That nets the winter sun beyond my sliding windows,
I notice that all the telegraph poles along the lane
Are waggling convulsively, and the wires
Bounce like skipping-ropes round flustered birds.
The earth creeps under the floor. A cherry tree
Agitates itself outside, but it is no wind
That makes the long bamboo palisade
Begin to undulate down all its length.

The clock stammers and stops. There is a queer racket,
Like someone rapping on the wooden walls,
Then through the ceiling's falling flakes I see
The brass handles on a high chest of drawers
Dithering and dancing in a brisk distraction.
The lamp swings like a headache, and the whole house
Rotates slightly on grinding rollers.
Smoothly, like a spoilt child putting out a tongue,
A drawer shoots half-out, and quietly glides back again,
Closed with a snap of teeth, a sharper click
Than such a casual grimace prepared me for.

The stove-pipe's awkward elbow
Twangles its three supporting wires. Doors
Slam, fly open: my quiet maid erupts from
Nowhere, blushing furiously, yet smiling wildly
As if to explain, excuse, console and warn.
Together, like lost children in a fairy-tale
Who escape from an enchanter's evil cottage,
We rush out into the slightly unbalanced garden. A pole
Vibrates still like a plucked bass string,
But the ground no longer squirms beneath our feet,
And the trees are composing themselves, have birds again.

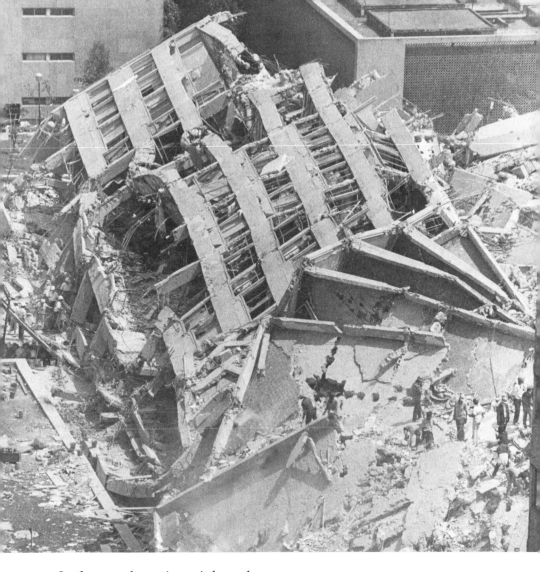

In the spooky quiet, a 'plane drones
Like a metal top, and though the sound
Gives a sense of disaster averted,
And is even oddly re-assuring, as
The pulse of confident engines,
Throbbing high above an electric storm, can comfort,
We feel that somewhere out of sight
Something has done its worst. Meanwhile,
The house tries to look as if nothing had happened,
And over the roof's subtle curves
Lets the flamingo-coloured kite fly undisturbed.

JAMES KIRKUP

An Island In The City

An island in the city, happy demolition men
behind windowed hoardings—look at them
trailing drills through rubble dust, kicking rubble,
smoking leaning on a pick, putting the stub
over an ear and the hot yellow helmet over that,
whistling up the collapsing chimney, kicking the
ricochet, rattling the trail with
snakes of wire, slamming slabs
down, plaster, cornice, brick, brick
on broken brick and plaster dust,
sprawling with steaming cans and pieces
at noon, afternoon bare sweat shining
paths down chalky backs, coughing
in filtered sunshine, slithering, swearing,
joking, slowly stacking and building
their rubbish into a total bonfire.
Look at that Irishman, bending
in a beautiful arc to throw
the last black rafter to the top,
stands back, walks round it singing
as it crackles into flame—old doors,
old beams, boxes, window-frames,
a rag doll, sacks, flex, old newspapers,
burst shelves, a shoe, old dusters, rags of
wallpaper roses. And they all stand round,
and cheer the tenement to smoke.

EDWIN MORGAN

The Pond

With nets and kitchen sieves they raid the pond,
Chasing the minnows into bursts of mud,
Scooping and chopping, raking up frond after frond
Of swollen weed after a week of flood.

Thirty or forty minnows bob and flash
In every jam-jar hoarded on the edge,
While the shrill children with each ill-aimed splash
Haul out another dozen as they dredge.

Choked to its banks, the pond spills out its store
Of frantic life. Nothing can drain it dry
Of what it breeds: it breeds so effortlessly
Theft seems to leave it richer than before.

The nostrils snuff its rank bouquet—how warm,
How lavish, foul, and indiscriminate, fat
With insolent appetite and thirst, so that
The stomach almost heaves to see it swarm.

But trapped in glass the minnows flail and fall,
Sink, with upended bellies showing white.
After an hour I look and see that all
But four or five have died. The greenish light

Ripples to stillness, while the children bend
To spoon the corpses out, matter-of-fact,
Absorbed: as if creation's prodigial act
Shrank to this empty jam-jar in the end.

ANTHONY THWAITE

Going Away and Returning

The best of going away is the going—
That inland sea view
Glimpsed through gaps in a traffic queue;
White mosques on stilts of a pier striding
Towards empty horizons blue with dreaming.

Jolted, we arrive
At Bella Vista gleaming
Gull-grey on a grey parade
Where tired waves at high-tide flap-
Flop, slopping on grey stones.

Later the swept shore is sad
With deck-chair sleepers, paddling children, mad
Mothers grabbing their infants from the sea,
Couples linked by hoarse transistors,
Picnic-papers,
Castles built to be washed away,
And shells,
Scoured, gathered, taken home
To a blind house that smells
Of lack and damp.

Return is dead flowers
In the same vase;
That letter unanswered on the fridge;
Floor unswept;
Clock stopped; range
Cold—the worst of coming back is the kept
Secret of a locked house,
Ourselves on the outside, strange.

PHOEBE HESKETH

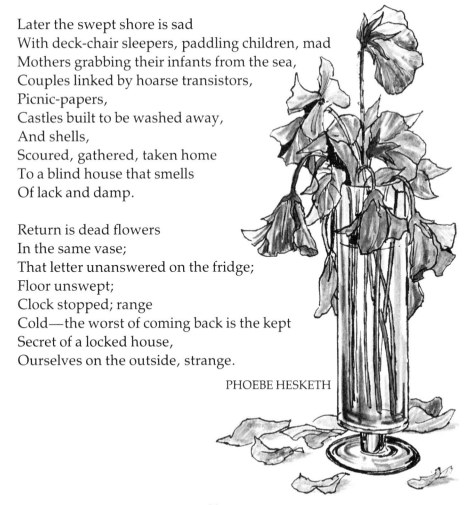

Tea in a Space-Ship

In this world a tablecloth need not be laid
On any table, but is spread out anywhere
Upon the always equidistant and
Invisible legs of gravity's wild air.

The tea, which never would grow cold,
Gathers itself into a wet and steaming ball,
And hurls its liquid molecules at anybody's head,
Or dances, eternal bilboquet,
In and out of the suspended cups up-
Ended in the weightless hands
Of chronically nervous jerks
Who yet would never spill a drop,
Their mouths agape for passing cakes.

Lumps of sparkling sugar
Sling themselves out of their crystal bowl
With a disordered fountain's
Ornamental stops and starts.
The milk describes a permanent parabola
Girdled with satellites of spinning tarts.

The future lives with graciousness.
The hostess finds her problems eased,
For there is honey still for tea
And butter keeps the ceiling greased.

She will provide, of course,
No cake-forks, spoons or knives.
They are so sharp, so dangerously gadabout,
It is regarded as a social misdemeanour
To put them out.

JAMES KIRKUP

94

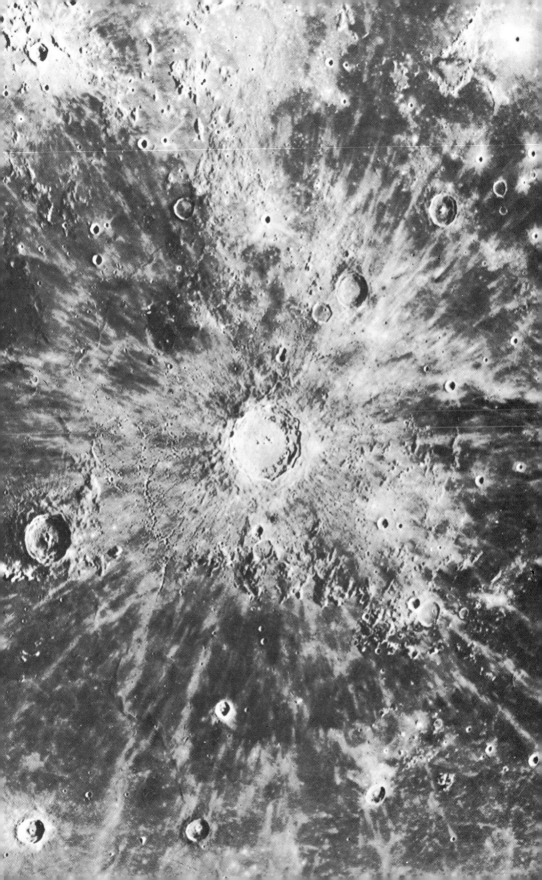

Space Shot

Out of the furnace
The great fish rose
Its silver tail on fire
But with a slowness
Like something sorry
To be rid of earth.
The boiling mountains
Of snow white cloud
Searched for a space to go into
And the ground thundered
With a roar
That set teacups
Rattling in a kitchen
Twenty miles away.
Across the blue it arched
Milk bottle white
But shimmering in the haze.
And the watchers by the fence
Held tinted glass against their eyes
And wondered at what man could do
To make so large a thing
To fly so far and free.
While the unknown Universe waited;
For waiting
Was what it had always been good at.

GARETH OWEN

Welsh Incident

'But that was nothing to what things came out
From the sea-caves of Criccieth yonder.'
'What were they? Mermaids? dragons? ghosts?'
'Nothing at all of any things like that,'
'What were they, then?
                            'All sorts of queer things,
Things never seen or heard or written about,
Very strange, un-Welsh, utterly peculiar
Things. Oh, solid enough they seemed to touch,
Had anyone dared it. Marvellous creation,
All various shapes and sizes and no sizes,
All new, each perfectly unlike his neighbour,
Though all came moving slowly out together.'
'Describe just one of them.'
                            'I am unable.'
'What were their colours?'
                            'Mostly nameless colours,
Colours you'd like to see; but one was puce
Or perhaps more like crimson, but not purplish.
Some had no colour.'
                        'Tell me, had they legs?'
'Not a leg nor foot among them that I saw.'
'But did these things come out in any order?
What o'clock was it? What was the day of the week?
Who else was present? How was the weather?'
'I was coming to that. It was half-past three
On Easter Tuesday last. The sun was shining.
The Harlech Silver Band played *Marchog Jesu*
On thirty-seven shimmering instruments,
Collecting for Carnarvon's (Fever) Hospital Fund.
The populations of Pwllheli, Criccieth,
Portmadoc, Borth, Tremadoc, Penrhyndeudraeth,
Were all assembled. Criccieth's major addressed them
First in good Welsh and then in fluent English,
Twisting his fingers in his chain of office,
Welcoming the things. They came out on the sand,
Not keeping time to the band, moving seaward

Silently at a snail's pace. But at last
The most odd, indescribable thing of all,
Which hardly one man there could see for wonder,
Did something recognizably a something.'
'Well, what?'
                'It made a noise.'
                           'A frightening noise?'
'No, no.'
           'A musical noise? A noise of scuffling?'
'No, but a very loud, respectable noise—
Like groaning to oneself on Sunday morning
In Chapel, close before the second psalm.'
'What did the mayor do?'
                     'I was coming to that.'

                          ROBERT GRAVES

Slough

Come, friendly bombs, and fall on Slough
It isn't fit for humans now,
There isn't grass to graze a cow
    Swarm over, Death!

Come, bombs, and blow to smithereens
Those air-conditioned, bright canteens,
Tinned fruit, tinned meat, tinned milk, tinned beans
    Tinned minds, tinned breath.

Mess up the mess they call a town—
A house for ninety-seven down
And once a week a half-a-crown
    For twenty years.

And get the man with double chin
Who'll always cheat and always win,
Who washes his repulsive skin
    In women's tears.

And smash his desk of polished oak
And smash his hands so used to stroke
And stop his boring dirty joke
    And make him yell.

But spare the bald young clerks who add
The profits of the stinking cad;
It's not their fault that they are mad,
    They've tasted Hell.

It's not their fault they do not know
The birdsong from the radio,
It's not their fault they often go
    To Maidenhead

And talk of sports and makes of cars
In various bogus Tudor bars
And daren't look up and see the stars
    But belch instead.

In labour-saving homes, with care
Their wives frizz out peroxide hair
And dry it in synthetic air
    And paint their nails.

Come, friendly bombs, and fall on Slough
To get it ready for the plough.
The cabbages are coming now:
    The earth exhales.

JOHN BETJEMAN

Talking and writing. Night has its own special atmosphere. Most of you will have lain awake at some time aware of the sounds and shapes in the darkness about you.

What sort of sounds do you notice?

Can you think of any words or comparisons to describe the darkness?

Usually you can make out some shapes. What do they remind you of? What are your feelings?

Perhaps some light comes in from outside from the street-lights, the moon, or from car headlights. Can you find words or comparisons to describe its effect?

You may be able to write a poem from one of these ideas.

Haiku. Attics and cellars are often strange and rarely visited parts of houses. Your own home may have them or you may have visited a house which has. Jot down quickly some of the things that you see there and try to capture the atmosphere of the place in a poem.

You may find it concentrates your ideas to focus on just one thought and to capture it as a haiku poem. (Look back to page 8 if you want to refresh your memory about haiku.)

Picture into poem. Look at the photograph of the moon's surface on page 95. Write down quickly as many words, phrases and comparisons as you can to describe its appearance. When you have finished your notes you may be able to use them as the basis for a poem entitled 'Moon Landing' in which you imagine the last stages of a spacecraft's descent to the moon's surface. How does the appearance of the moon change as you get closer? It may help you to imagine yourself falling into the photograph.

Performing. Robert Graves' poem *Welsh Incident* on page 98 is in the form of a strange conversation between a very Welsh voice that tells the story of what happened and another—maybe English —questioner. It needs to be performed by two people who aren't afraid to read it very seriously with the right accents. Like a shaggy dog story it never really gets anywhere: it's the way you tell it that matters!

Talking and performing. John Betjeman who wrote *Slough* (page 99) was a great admirer of Victorian buildings and hated very modern developments in both architecture and manners. His lament over what he sees as the destruction of a town he once liked may strike you as unfair, overdone, snobbish even—or you may find you share some of his anger. In groups, divide the poem up and perform a reading of it using different voices for different verses. What do *you* think? Has Betjeman got a point?

Poem and picture. Edwin Morgan's poem *An Island in The City* on page 91 is a picture in words. It's full of details describing the demolition site which is like a busy island in the middle of the city buildings. Either try to conjure up a busy scene in your mind's eye—perhaps a crowded shop or market, a bus station, a holiday beach . . . and bring it alive in words in a similar way (notice the way Edwin Morgan uses words like 'trailing', 'kicking', 'leaning', 'whist-ling', 'slamming' . . . to make you see it happening *now*) *or* turn the poem back into a picture and draw or paint an illustration to go alongside the original poem.

SEASONS

'The Fight of the Year'

'And there goes the bell for the third month
and Winter comes out of its corner looking groggy
Spring leads with a left to the head
followed by a sharp right to the body
    daffodils
    primroses
    crocuses
    snowdrops
    lilacs
    violets
    pussywillow
Winter can't take much more punishment
and Spring shows no signs of tiring
    tadpoles
    squirrels
    baalambs
    badgers
    bunny rabbits
    mad march hares
    horses and hounds
Spring is merciless
Winter won't go the full twelve rounds
    bobtail clouds
    scallywaggy winds
    the sun
    a pavement artist
    in every town
A left to the chin
and Winter's down!

1 tomatoes
2 radish
3 cucumber
4 onions
5 beetroot
6 celery
7 and any
8 amount
9 of lettuce
10 for dinner
Winter's out for the count
Spring is the winner!'

ROGER McGOUGH

Spring

To pass by a pondbrink
Trodden by horses
Where among the green horsetails
Even the hoofprints
Shiver with tadpoles
Comma'ed with offspring
And moist buds flick awake
On breeze-floundering sallows.

PETER REDGROVE

March

Awake to the cold light
of wet wind running
twigs in tremors. Walls
are naked. Twilights raw—
and when the sun taps steeples
their glistenings dwindle
upward . . .

       March
slips along the ground
like a mouse under pussy
willows, a little hungry.

The vagrant ghost of winter,
is it this that keeps the chimney
busy still? For something still
nudges shingles and windows:

but waveringly,—this ghost,
this slate-eyed saintly wraith
of winter wanes
and knows its waning.

HART CRANE

May Day

The whole county apparently afloat:
Every road bridging or skirting water,
The land islanded, lough and burn turned moat.

That bulrush at attention. I had to
Wade barefoot over spongy, ice-cold marsh
(No bottom, just water seeping through

The netted weed) to get near where it stood
Perennially dry among May blossoming,
Chalky, velvety, rooted in liquid.

The elements running to watercolour,
The skyline filled up to the very brim.
The globe was flooded inwardly, fuller

Than a melon, the rind not even solid
For remember, in a ditch, the unstanched spring
Flushing itself all over the road.

SEAMUS HEANEY

Season

Rust is ripeness, rust
And the wilted corn-plume;
Pollen is mating-time when swallows
Weave a dance
Of feathered arrows
Thread corn-stalks in winged
Streaks of light. And, we loved to hear
Spliced phrases of the wind, to hear
Rasps in the field, where corn leaves
Pierce like bamboo slivers.

Now, garnerers we,
Awaiting rust on tassels, draw
Long shadows from the dusk, wreathe
Dry thatch in woodsmoke. Laden stalks
Ride the germ's decay—we await
The promise of the rust.

WOLE SOYINKA

July

. . . noon burns with its blistering breath
Around, and day dies still as death.
The busy noise of man and brute
Is on a sudden lost and mute;
Even the brook that leaps along
Seems weary of its bubbling song,
And, so soft its waters creep,
Tired silence sinks in sounder sleep.
The very flies forget to hum;
And, save the waggon rocking round,
The landscape sleeps without a sound.
The breeze is stopt, the lazy bough
Hath not a leaf that dances now;
The totter-grass upon the hill,
And spiders' threads, are standing still;
The feathers dropt from moor-hen's wing,
Which to the water's surface cling,
Are steadfast, and as heavy seem
As stones beneath them in the stream;
Hawkweed and groundsel's fanning downs
Unruffled keep their seedy crowns;
And in the oven-heated air,
Not one light thing is floating there,
Save that to the earnest eye,
The restless heat seems twittering by.

From The Shepherd's Calendar

JOHN CLARE

To Autumn

I

Season of mists and mellow fruitfulness,
   Close bosom-friend of the maturing sun;
Conspiring with him how to load and bless
   With fruit the vines that round the thatch-eaves run;
To bend with apples the moss'd cottage-trees,
   And fill all fruit with ripeness to the core;
     To swell the gourd, and plump the hazel shells
   With a sweet kernel; to set budding more,
And still more, later flowers for the bees,
Until they think warm days will never cease,
     For Summer has o'er-brimmed their clammy cells.

II

Who hath not seen thee oft amid thy store?
   Sometimes whoever seeks abroad may find
Thee sitting careless on a granary floor,
   Thy hair soft-lifted by the winnowing wind;
Or on a half-reaped furrow sound asleep,
   Drows'd with the fume of poppies, while thy hook
     Spares the next swath and all its twined flowers:
And sometimes like a gleaner thou dost keep
   Steady thy laden head across a brook;
   Or by a cyder-press, with patient look,
     Thou watchest the last oozings hours by hours.

III

Where are the songs of Spring? Ah, where are they?
   Think not of them, thou hast thy music too,—
While barred clouds bloom the soft-dying day,
   And touch the stubble-plains with rosy hue;
Then in a wailful choir the small gnats mourn
   Among the river sallows, borne aloft
     Or sinking as the light wind lives or dies;
And full-grown lambs loud bleat from hilly bourn;
   Hedge-crickets sing; and now with treble soft
   The red-breast whistles from a garden-croft;
     And gathering swallows twitter in the skies.

JOHN KEATS

Autumn

I love the fitful gust that shakes
The casement all the day,
And from the glossy elm-tree takes
The faded leaves away,
Twirling them by the window pane
With thousand others down the lane.

I love to see the shaking twig
Dance till the shut of eve,
The sparrow on the cottage rig,
Whose chirp would make believe
That Spring was just now flirting by
In Summer's lap with flowers to lie.

I love to see the cottage smoke
Curl upwards through the trees,
The pigeons nestled round the cote
On November days like these:
The cock upon the dunghill crowing,
The mill-sails on the heath a-going.

The feather from the raven's breast
Falls on the stubble lea,
The acorns near the old crow's nest
Drop pattering down the tree:
The grunting pigs that wait for all,
Scramble and hurry where they fall.

JOHN CLARE

October Dawn

October is marigold, and yet
A glass half full of wine left out

To the dark heaven all night, by dawn
Has dreamed a premonition

Of ice across its eye as if
The ice-age had begun its heave.

The lawn overtrodden and strewn
From the night before, and the whistling green

Shrubbery are doomed. Ice
Has got its spearhead into place.

First a skin, delicately here
Restraining a ripple from the air;

Soon plate and rivet upon pond and brook;
Then tons of chain and massive lock

To hold rivers. Then, sound by sight
Will Mammoth and Sabre-tooth celebrate

Reunion while a fist of cold
Squeezes the fire at the core of the world,

Squeezes the fire at the core of the heart,
And now it is about to start.

TED HUGHES

Skating

From *The Prelude*

And in the frosty season, when the sun
Was set, and visible for many a mile
The cottage windows blazed through twilight gloom,
I heeded not their summons: happy time
It was indeed for all of us—for me
It was a time of rapture! Clear and loud
The village clock tolled six,—I wheeled about,
Proud and exulting like an untired horse
That cares not for his home. All shod with steel,
We hissed along the polished ice in games
Confederate, imitative of the chase
And woodland pleasures,—the resounding horn,
The pack loud chiming, and the hunted hare.
So through the darkness and the cold we flew,
And not a voice was idle; with the din
Smitten, the precipices rang aloud;
The leafless trees and every icy crag
Tinkled like iron; while far distant hills
Into the tumult sent an alien sound
Of melancholy not unnoticed, while the stars
Eastward were sparkling clear, and in the west
The orange sky of evening died away.
Not seldom from the uproar I retired
Into a silent bay, or sportively
Glanced sideways, leaving the tumultuous throng,
To cut across the reflex of a star
That fled, and, flying still before me, gleamed
Upon the glassy plain; and oftentimes,
When we had given our bodies to the wind,
And all the shadowy banks on either side
Came sweeping through the darkness, spinning still
The rapid line of motion, then at once
Have I, reclining back upon my heels,

Stopped short; yet still the solitary cliffs
Wheeled by me—even as if the earth had rolled
With visible motion her diurnal round!
Behind me did they stretch in solemn train,
Feebler and feebler, and I stood and watched
Till all was tranquil as a dreamless sleep.

WILLIAM WORDSWORTH

Ice

The North Wind sighed:
And in a trice
What was water
Now is ice.

What sweet rippling
Water was
Now bewitched is
Into glass:

White and brittle
Where is seen
The prisoned milfoil's
Tender green;

Clear and ringing,
With sun aglow,
Where the boys sliding
And skating go.

Now furred's each stick
And stalk and blade
With crystals out of
Dewdrops made.

Worms and ants
Flies, snails and bees
Keep close house-guard,
Lest they freeze;

Oh, with how sad
And solemn an eye
Each fish stares up
Into the sky.

In dread lest his
Wide watery home
At night shall solid
Ice become.

WALTER DE LA MARE

Weatherman

I am de weatherman
and dere's no dreaderman
in English company
than de weatherman
and dat's me

I am de weatherman
de ghost at every conversation
rising higher than inflation
de shadow across your day
controlling your destiny
with visions of grey

I am de weatherman
I come dancing out of thin air
to send my chilly breath
down the reaches of your ear and neck
and dere's nothing your thermal vest
could do about it you hear

I am de weatherman
your friendly prophet of doom
de eternal conversation piece
but occasionally I make room
for football results and British Leyland

I am de weatherman
standing back with professional ease
smiling a sweet 2 degrees
below zero smile
because I'm a sadist at heart
and enjoy watching you freeze

I am de weatherman
grinning behind scattered showers
de mastermind of atmosphere
and my allies are everywhere

neatly dressed invisible powers
disguised as that fellow passenger
who never ever remembers
to close a train door
that thoughtful person
with one eye on the skies
who always carries an umbrella
just in case
just in case
just in case

I am de weatherman
and like the phoenix I rise
from the foggy ashes
of the 9 o'clock news
proclaiming my northwesterly blues
so better get on your non-slip shoes

I am de weatherman
de sore thumb in your diary
de frosty finger on your spine
because I'm allergic to sunshine

I am de man
to make de taxman
tremble for a taxfree touch of sun
I am de man
to make President Reagan
reach for his gun
I am de man
to make de Iron Lady
reach for her cardigun

Yes I am de weatherman
and dere's no dreaderman
no dreaderman
no dreaderman

JOHN AGARD

List poem. What details come to mind when you think of each of the four seasons?

Jot down, in rough, the phrase 'Spring is . . .' as the beginning of your poem. Now, try to write down *quickly* (each on a separate line) the sights, sounds, smells and activities which this season brings to mind.

Try to make similar notes for the other three seasons. Do not spend more than three or four minutes on each: treat it like a brainstorming session.

Use your notes as the basis for a short poem. Can your ideas be put together with those of others in the class to make a longer group poem?

Writing. In the piece on page 112 Wordsworth conveys the excitement he felt when skating late into the winter evening. Try to capture *your* feelings when you are sledging, snowballing, sliding, skating or skiing. What do you hear? and see? how do you move and breathe? what are your feelings—fear? excitement? delight? . . .

Haiku. The seasons are a traditional source of inspiration for haiku poems, partly because they provide many simple, striking images.

Perhaps you could write a haiku suggested by one of the following: the winter sun; winter trees; warm summer rain; first spring shoots (the picture on page 11 may help); holly berries; fields of stubble.

If you are in doubt about the haiku form look back at page 8.

Performing. Roger McGough takes the well known sports' commentator's phrase 'The Fight of the Year' quite literally in his poem on page 103. It's a poem to perform; in groups or as a whole class you could give it all you've got. One voice is the commentator and the whole group 'counts the year out' at different points.

Performing. John Agard knows and is amused by the way the weather crops up in so many conversations in England, and how people anxiously watch the weather forecast. Divide the lines of the poem on page 115 between several 'weathermen'—one for each verse—and, using different voices, make a lively performance out of his teasing.

CREATURES

The Fish

I caught a tremendous fish
and held him beside the boat
half out of water, with my hook
fast in the corner of his mouth.
He didn't fight.
He hadn't fought at all.
He hung a grunting weight,
battered and venerable
and homely. Here and there
his brown skin hung in strips
like ancient wall-paper,
and its pattern of darker brown
was like wall-paper:
shapes like full-blown roses
stained and lost through age.
He was speckled with barnacles,
fine rosettes of lime,
and infested
with tiny white sea-lice,
and underneath two or three
rags of green weed hung down.
While his gills were breathing in
the terrible oxygen
—the frightening gills
fresh and crisp with blood,
that can cut so badly—
I thought of the coarse white flesh
packed in like feathers,
the big bones and the little bones,

119

the dramatic reds and blacks
of his shiny entrails,
and the pink swim-bladder
like a big peony.
I looked into his eyes
which were far larger than mine
but shallower, and yellowed,
the irises backed and packed
with tarnished tinfoil
seen through the lenses
of old scratched isinglass.
They shifted a little, but not
to return my stare.
—It was more like the tipping
of an object toward the light.
I admired his sullen face,
the mechanism of his jaw,
and then I saw
that from his lower lip
—if you could call it a lip—
grim, wet and weapon-like,
hung five old pieces of fish-line,
or four and a wire leader
with the swivel still attached,

with all their five big hooks
grown firmly in his mouth.
A green line, frayed at the end
where he broke it, two heavier lines,
and a fine black thread
still crimped from the strain and snap
when it broke and he got away.
Like medals with their ribbons
frayed and wavering
a five-haired beard of wisdom
trailing from his aching jaw.
I stared and stared
and victory filled up
the little rented boat,
from the pool of bilge
where oil had spread a rainbow
around the rusted engine,
to the bailer rusted orange,
the sun-cracked thwarts,
the oarlocks on their strings,
the gunnels—until everything
was rainbow, rainbow, rainbow!
And I let the fish go.

ELIZABETH BISHOP

Old Wolf

lopes on purpose, paddling the snow
Of the soft-blown winterlocked landscape,
Under the loaded branches in the hush of forests.
Stops for its own reasons, shapeless
In the white shadows that have
Stopped breathing.
The prints run into the dark and
The stars wheel, circling the silence.

JAMES TAYLOR

The Runaway

Once when the snow of the year was beginning to fall,
We stopped by a mountain pasture to say, 'Whose colt?'
A little Morgan had one forefoot on the wall,
The other curled at his breast. He dipped his head
And snorted at us. And then he had to bolt.
We heard the miniature thunder where he fled,
And we saw him, or thought we saw him, dim and grey,
Like a shadow against the curtain of falling flakes.
'I think the little fellow's afraid of the snow.
He isn't winter-broken. It isn't play
With the little fellow at all. He's running away.
I doubt if even his mother could tell him, "Sakes,
It's only weather," He'd think she didn't know!
Where is his mother? He can't be out alone.'
And now he comes again with clatter of stone,
And mounts the wall again with whited eyes
And all his tail that isn't hair up straight.
He shudders his coat as if to throw off flies.
'Whoever it is that leaves him out so late,
When other creatures have gone to stall and bin,
Ought to be told to come and take him in.'

ROBERT FROST

A Bird Came Down the Walk

A bird came down the walk:
He did not know I saw;
He bit an angle-worm in halves
And ate the fellow, raw.

And then he drank a dew
From a convenient grass,
And then hopped sidewise to the wall
To let a beetle pass.

He glanced with rapid eyes
That hurried all abroad,—
They looked like frightened beads, I thought
He stirred his velvet head

Like one in danger; cautious,
I offered him a crumb,
And he unrolled his feathers
And rowed him softer home

Than oars divide the ocean,
Too silver for a seam,
Or butterflies, off banks of noon,
Leap, plashless, as they swim.

EMILY DICKINSON

Rookery

Here they come, freckling the sunset,
The slow big sailers bearing down
On the plantation. They have flown
Their sorties and are now well met.

The upper twigs dip and wobble
With each almost two-point landing,
Then ride to rest. There is nothing
Else to do now only settle.

But they keep up a guttural chat
As stragglers knock the roost see-saw.
Something's satisfied in that caw.
Who wouldn't come to rest like that?

SEAMUS HEANEY

The Fly

Little Fly,
Thy summer's play
My thoughtless hand
Has brushed away.

Am not I
A fly like thee?
Or art not thou
A man like me?

For I dance,
And drink, and sing,
Till some blind hand
Shall brush my wing.

If thought is life
And strength and breath,
And the want
Of thought is death;

Then am I
A happy fly,
If I live
Or if I die.

WILLIAM BLAKE

Aid

I almost popped underfoot
A shiny beetle like a boot
Its laces waving in the air
Not knowing how it was or where:
Being drunk, I had the knack
To know its feelings on its back;
I'd get my foot under its carapace
And shove it safely back to grass:
It might want to get there quick
To the damp grass to be sick
Or, plates creaking, unload its eggs.
I stood unsteady on my bottled legs
And raised one foot, as I have said:
But, to keep my balance, squashed its head.

Looking down, I held my breath
At this accidental death;
Scanning up and down the path,
I waited for descending wrath;
Then, keeping the ground beneath my feet
I strolled off home to eat,
Along the stony paths, leaf-strewn,
Whistling a sober little tune.

PETER REDGROVE

View of a Pig

The pig lay on a barrow dead.
It weighed, they said, as much as three men.
Its eyes closed, pink white eyelashes.
Its trotters stuck straight out.

Such weight and thick pink bulk
Set in death seemed not just dead.
It was less than lifeless, further off.
It was like a sack of wheat.

126

I thumped it without feeling remorse.
One feels guilty insulting the dead,
Walking on graves. But this pig
Did not seem able to accuse.

It was too dead. Just so much
A poundage of lard and pork.
Its last dignity had entirely gone.
It was not a figure of fun.

Too dead now to pity.
To remember its life, din, stronghold
Of earthly pleasure as it had been,
Seemed a false effort, and off the point.

Too deadly factual. Its weight
Oppressed me—how could it be moved?
And the trouble of cutting it up!
The gash in its throat was shocking, but not pathetic.

Once I ran at a fair in the noise
To catch a greased piglet
That was faster and nimbler than a cat,
Its squeal was the rending of metal.

Pigs must have hot blood, they feel like ovens.
Their bite is worse than a horse's—
They chop a half-moon clean out.
They eat cinders, dead cats.

Distinctions and admirations such
As this one was long finished with.
I stared at it a long time. They were going to scald it,
Scald it and scour it like a doorstep.

TED HUGHES

127

Dissection

This rat looks like it is made of marzipan
Soft and neatly packaged in its envelope;
I shake it free.
Fingering the damp, yellow fur, I know
That this first touch is far the worst.
   There is a book about it that contains
Everything on a rat, with diagrams
Meticulous, but free from blood
Or all the yellow juices
I will have to pour away.
   Now peg it out:
My pins are twisted and the board is hard
But, using force and fracturing its legs
I manage though
And crucify my rat.
   From the crutch to the throat the fur is ripped
Not neatly, not as shown in the diagrams,
But raggedly;
My hacking has revealed the body wall
As a sack that is fat with innards to be torn
By the inquisitive eye
And the hand that strips aside.
   Inside this taut, elastic sack is a surprise;
Not the chaos I had thought to find,
No oozing mash; instead of that
A firmly coiled discipline
Of overlapping liver, folded gut;
A neatness that is like a small machine—
And I wonder what it is that has left this rat,
Why a month of probing could not make it go again,
What it is that has disappeared . . .
   The bell has gone; it is time to go for lunch.
I fold the rat, replace it in its bag,
Wash from my hands the sweet
Smell of meat and formalin
And go and eat a meat pie afterwards.
   So, for four weeks or so, I am told

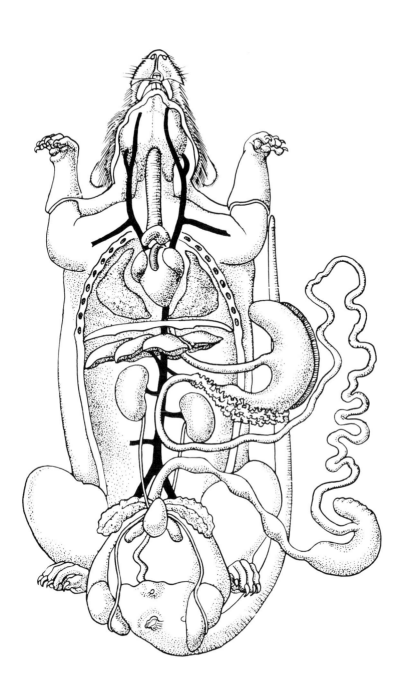

I shall continue to dissect this rat;
Like a child
Pulling apart a clock he cannot mend.

COLIN ROWBOTHAM

An Advancement of Learning

I took the embankment path
(As always, deferring
The bridge). The river nosed past,
Pliable, oil-skinned, wearing

A transfer of gables and sky.
Hunched over the railing,
Well away from the road now, I
Considered the dirty-keeled swans.

Something slobbered curtly, close,
Smudging the silence: a rat
Slimed out of the water and
My throat sickened so quickly that

I turned down the path in cold sweat
But God, another was nimbling
Up the far bank, tracing its wet
Arcs on the stones. Incredibly then

I established a dreaded
Bridgehead. I turned to stare
With deliberate, thrilled care
At my hitherto snubbed rodent.

He clockworked aimlessly a while,
Stopped, back bunched and glistening,
Ears plastered down on his knobbed skull,
Insidiously listening.

The tapered tail that followed him,
The raindrop eye, the old snout:
One by one I took all in.
He trained on me. I stared him out

Forgetting how I used to panic
When his grey brothers scraped and fed
Behind the hen-coop in our yard,
On ceiling boards above my bed.

This terror, cold, wet-furred, small-clawed,
Retreating up a pipe for sewage.
I stared a minute after him.
Then I walked on and crossed the bridge.

SEAMUS HEANEY

Cats

Cats are contradictions; tooth and claw
Velvet-padded;
Snowflake-gentle paw
A fist of pins;
Kettles on the purr
Ready to spit;
Black silk then bristled fur.

Cats are of the East—
Scimitar and sphinx;
Sunlight striped with shade.
Leopard, lion, lynx
Moss-footed in a frightened glade;
Slit-eyes an amber glint
Or boring through the darkness, cool as jade.

Cats have come to rest
Upon the cushioned West.
Here, dyed-in-the-silk,
They lap up bottled milk—
Not that of human kindness—
And return
To the mottled woods of Spring
Making the trees afraid
With leaf and wing
A-flutter at the movement in the fern.

Midnight-wild
With phosphorescent eyes,
Cats are morning-wise
Sleeping as they stare into the sun,
Blind to the light,
Deaf to echoing cries
From a ravaged wood.
Cats see black and white
Morning and night as one.

PHOEBE HESKETH

Cats

Cats no less liquid than their shadows
Offer no angles to the wind.
They slip, diminished, neat, through loopholes
Less than themselves; will not be pinned

To rules or routes for journeys; counter
Attack with non-resistance; twist
Enticing through the curving fingers
And leave an angered, empty fist.

They wait, obsequious as darkness
Quick to retire, quick to return;
Admit no aim or ethics; flatter
With reservations; will not learn

To answer to their names; are seldom
Truly owned till shot or skinned.
Cats no less liquid than their shadows
Offer no angles to the wind.

A. S. J. TESSIMOND

My Cat Jeoffry

For I will consider my cat Jeoffry.

For he is the servant of the Living God, duly and daily serving Him.

For at the first glance of the Glory of God in the East he worships in his way.

For is this done by wreathing his body seven times round with elegant quickness.

For then he leaps up to catch the musk, which is the blessing of God on his prayer.

For he rolls upon prank to work it in.

For having done duty, and received blessing, he begins to consider himself.

For this he performs in ten degrees.

For first he looks upon his forepaws to see if they are clean.

For secondly he kicks up behind to clear away there.

For thirdly he works it upon stretch with the forepaws extended.

For fourthly he sharpens his paws by wood.

For fifthly he washes himself.

For sixthly he rolls upon wash.

For seventhly he fleas himself, that he may not be interrupted upon the beat.

For eighthly he rubs himself a-gainst a post.

For ninthly he looks up for his instructions.

For tenthly he goes in quest of food.

For having considered God and himself he will consider his neighbour.

For if he meets another cat he will kiss her in kindness.

For when he takes his prey he plays with it to give it a chance.

For one mouse in seven escapes by his dallying.

For when his day's work is done his business more properly begins.

For he keeps the Lord's watch in the night against the Adversary.

For he counteracts the powers of darkness by his electrical skin and glaring eyes.

For he counteracts the Devil, who is death, by brisking about
the life.

For in his morning orisons he loves the sun and the sun loves
him.

For he is of the tribe of Tiger.

For the Cherub Cat is a term of the Angel Tiger.

For he has the subtlety and hiss of the serpent, which in
goodness he suppresses.

For he will not do destruction, if he is well-fed, neither will
he spit without provocation.

For he purrs in thankfulness, when God tells him he's a good
Cat.

For he is an instrument for the children to learn benevolence
upon.

For every house is incomplete without him and a blessing is
lacking in the spirit.

For the Lord commanded Moses concerning the cats at the
departure of the Children of Israel from Egypt.

For every family had one cat at least in the bag.

For the English cats are the best in Europe.

For he is the cleanest in the use of his forepaws of any
quadrupede.

For the dexterity of his defence is an instance of the love of
God to him exceedingly.

For he is the quickest to his mark of any creature.

For he is tenacious of his point.

For he is a mixture of gravity and waggery.

For he knows that God is his Saviour.

For there is nothing sweeter than his peace when at rest.

For there is nothing brisker than his life when in motion.

For he is of the Lord's poor and so indeed is he called by
benevolence perpetually—Poor Jeoffry! poor Jeoffry! the
rat has bit thy throat.

For I bless the name of the Lord Jesus that Jeoffry is better.

For the divine spirit comes about his body to sustain it in
complete cat.

For his tongue is exceeding pure so that it has in purity what
it wants in music.

For he is docile and can learn certain things.

For he can set up with gravity which is patience upon
    approbation.
For he can fetch and carry, which is patience in employment.
For he can jump over a stick which is patience upon proof
    positive.
For he can spraggle upon waggle at the word of command.
For he can jump from an eminence into his master's bosom.
For he can catch the cork and toss it again.
For he is hated by the hypocrite and miser.
For the former is afraid of detection.
And the latter refuses the charge.
For he camels his back to bear the first notion of business.
For he is good to think on, if a man would express himself
    neatly.
For he made a great figure in Egypt for his signal services.
For he killed the Ichneumon-rat very pernicious by land.
For his ears are so acute that they sting again.
For from this proceeds the passing quickness of his
    attention.
For by stroking of him I have found out electricity.
For I perceive God's light about him both wax and fire.
For the electrical fire is the spiritual substance, which God
    sends from heaven to sustain the bodies of both man and
    beast.
For God has blessed him in the variety of his movements.
For, tho he cannot fly, he is an excellent clamberer.
For his motions upon the face of the earth are more than any
    other quadrupede.
For he can tread to all the measures upon the music.
For he can swim for life.
For he can creep.

CHRISTOPHER SMART

136

Hawk

Things motionless were felt to move
    Downward; the hedges crawled
Down steep sun-molten banks to where
    The shrunken river sprawled:

Dark cloud-ravines of shadow flowed
    Sheer down the dark wood's cliff;
Draped heavily in golden heat,
    The limbs of air fell stiff:

And, threatening doom, the sky's concentrated will
Hung in one black speck, poised above the hill.

GEORGE ROSTREVOR HAMILTON

Upon the Snail

She goes but softly, but she goeth sure;
She stumbles not as stronger creatures do:
Her journey's shorter, so she may endure
Better than they which do much further go.

She makes no noise, but stilly seizeth on
The flower or herb appointed for her food,
The which she quietly doth feed upon,
While others range and gare, but find no good.

And though she doth but very softly go,
However 'tis not fast, nor slow, but sure;
And certainly they that do travel so,
The prize they do aim at, they do procure.

JOHN BUNYAN

Considering the Snail

The snail pushes through a green
night, for the grass is heavy
with water and meets over
the bright path he makes, where rain
has darkened the earth's dark. He
moves in a wood of desire,

pale antlers barely stirring
as he hunts. I cannot tell
what power is at work, drenched there
with purpose, knowing nothing.
What is a snail's fury? All
I think is that if later

I parted the blades above
the tunnel and saw the thin
trail of broken white across
litter, I would never have
imagined the slow passion
to that deliberate progress.

THOM GUNN

Looking closely. The three poems about cats on pages 132 to 135 each describe different ways of looking at these creatures. You yourself may have a cat; most of you, at one time or another, will have played with one, and you can probably suggest some reasons why people find them fascinating.

You may be able to write about one of the many different moods or habits of a cat: chasing a piece of string . . . playing with a ball . . . stalking a bird . . . lapping up milk . . . washing itself . . . sleeping . . . angry.

Whichever of these you choose, try to capture the details of the cat's movements, sounds, appearance, and feel of its fur.

Talking and writing. Many animals are hunters. You will all have watched such everyday occurrences as a blackbird after worms, a spider ensnaring a fly, a cat stalking a bird. Some of you may have seen rarer sights—a hawk swooping on its prey, a fox after chickens, a pike darting after smaller fish.

Working together in groups, discuss any incidents of this kind that you have seen. As you talk, jot down any words or phrases that seem to you to capture the *movement* of the creatures. (We have already used 'stalking', 'swooping', 'darting'). Now choose one incident yourself and describe in detail what you see in your mind's eye.

Picture into poem. On page 124 you will find a photograph of a bird feeding nestlings. In writing a poem suggested by this picture notice particularly the many small details of the nest, the feathers and foliage. The picture may also set you thinking about the way wild creatures struggle for survival.

Syllabic verse. Thom Gunn's Poem *Considering The Snail* on page 139 is an example of what is called *syllabic verse* in which each line has the same number of syllables. Here there are seven syllables to each line:

1   2 3 4   5   6 7
The snail pushes through a green

Try to write your own poem using syllabic verse.

SCHOOL

A Boy's Head

In it there is a space-ship
and a project
for doing away with piano lessons.

And there is
Noah's ark,
which shall be first.

And there is
an entirely new bird,
an entirely new hare,
an entirely new bumble-bee.

There is a river
that flows upwards.

There is a multiplication table.

There is anti-matter.

And it just cannot be trimmed.

I believe
that only what cannot be trimmed
is a head.
There is much promise
in the circumstance
that so many people have heads.

MIROSLAV HOLUB
(*trans. I. Milner and G. Theiner*)

Slow Reader

He can make sculptures
And fabulous machines
Invent games, tell jokes
Give solemn, adult advice
But he is slow to read.
When I take him on my knee
With his *Ladybird* book
He gazes into the air
Sighing and shaking his head
Like an old man
Who knows the mountains
Are impassable.

He toys with words
Letting them grow cold
As gristly meat
Until I relent
And let him wriggle free—
A fish returning
To its element
Or a white-eyed colt
Shying from the bit
As if he sees
That if he takes it
In his mouth
He'll never run
Quite free again.

VICKI FEAVER

Tich Miller

Tich Miller wore glasses
with elastoplast-pink frames
and had one foot three sizes larger than the other.

When they picked teams for outdoor games
she and I were always the last two
left standing by the wire-mesh fence.

We avoided one another's eyes,
stooping, perhaps, to re-tie a shoelace,
or affecting interest in the flight

of some fortunate bird, and pretended
not to hear the urgent conference:
'Have Tubby!' 'No, no, have Tich!'

Usually they chose me, the lesser dud,
and she lolloped, unselected,
to the back of the other team.

At eleven we went to different schools.
In time I learned to get my own back,
sneering at hockey-players who couldn't spell.

Tich died when she was twelve.

WENDY COPE

143

The Choosing

We were first equal Mary and I
with the same coloured ribbons in mouse-coloured hair,
and with equal shyness
we curtseyed to the lady councillor
for copies of Collins' Children's Classics.
First equal, equally proud.

Best friends too Mary and I
a common bond in being cleverest (equal)
in our small school's small class.
I remember
the competition for top desk
or to read aloud the lesson
at school service.
And my terrible fear
of her superiority at sums.

I remember the housing scheme
Where we both stayed.
The same house, different homes,
where the choices were made.

I don't know exactly why they moved,
but anyway they went.
Something about a three-apartment
and a cheaper rent.
But from the top deck of the high-school bus
I'd glimpse among the others on the corner
Mary's father, mufflered, contrasting strangely
with the elegant greyhounds by his side.
He didn't believe in high-school education,
especially for girls,
or in forking out for uniforms.

Ten years later on a Saturday—
I am coming home from the library—
sitting near me on the bus,
Mary
with a husband who is tall,
curly haired, has eyes
for no one else but Mary.
Her arms are round the full-shaped vase
that is her body.
Oh, you can see where the attraction lies
in Mary's life—
not that I envy her, really.

And I am coming from the library
with my arms full of books.
I think of the prizes that were ours for the taking
and wonder when the choices got made
we don't remember making.

LIZ LOCHHEAD

Last Lesson of the Afternoon

When will the bell ring, and end this weariness?
How long have they tugged the leash, and strained apart,
My pack of unruly hounds! I cannot start
Them again on a quarry of knowledge they hate to hunt,
I can haul them and urge them no more.

No longer now can I endure the brunt
Of the books that lie out on the desks; a full threescore
Of several insults of blotted pages, and scrawl
Of slovenly work that they have offered me.
I am sick, and what on earth is the good of it all?
What good to them or me, I cannot see!

        So, shall I take
My last dear fuel of life to heap on my soul
And kindle my will to a flame that shall consume
Their dross of indifference; and take the toll
Of their insults in punishment?—I will not!—

I will not waste my soul and my strength for this.
What do I care for all that they do amiss!
What is the point of this teaching of mine, and of this
Learning of theirs? It all goes down the same abyss.

What does it matter to me, if they can write
A description of a dog, or if they can't?
What is the point? To us both, it is all my aunt!
And yet I'm supposed to care, with all my might.

I do not, and will not; they won't and they don't;
   and that's all!
I shall keep my strength for myself; they can keep
   theirs as well.
Why should we beat our heads against the wall
Of each other? I shall sit and wait for the bell.

D. H. LAWRENCE

Term begins again (ostrich blues)

I find myself
in bed again
with the sheets up over
my head again

papers collect
on my desk again
reports and memos and lists again

there are the
timetables in black ink
again

the silhouetted heads
in rows against the light
again

the lists again
of books I haven't read
again

nightmares again
of assignations missed
again

of students riding off
on bicycles playing bass guitars
again

and I oversleep
              again
              and again

I find myself
in bed
again

with the sheets up over
my head

again

STEF PIXNER

TYPEWRITING CLASS

Dear Miss Hinson

I am spitting

In front of my top ratter

With the rest of my commercesnail sturdy students

Triping you this later.

The truce is Miss Hinson

I am not happy wiht my cross.

Every day on Woundsday

I sit in my dusk

With my type rutter

Trooping without lurking at the lattice

All sorts of weird messengers.

To give one exam pill,

'The quick down socks....

The quick brine pox.....

The sick frown box....

The sick down jocks

Humps over the hazy bog'

When everyone kows

That a sick down jock

Would not be seen dead

Near a hazy bog.

Another one we tripe is;

'Now is the tame

For all guide men

To cram to the head

Of the pratty.'

To may why of sinking

I that is all you get to tripe

In true whelks of sturdy

Then I am thinking of changing

To crookery classes.

I would sooner end up a crook

Than a shirt hand trappist

Any die of the wink.

I have taken the tremble, Miss Hinson

To trip you this later

So that you will be able

To understand my indignation.

I must clothe now

As the Bill is groaning

                    Yours fitfully.....

                         GARETH OWEN

149

Oh Bring Back Higher Standards

Oh bring back higher standards—
the pencil and the cane—
if we want education then we must have some pain.
Oh, bring us back all the gone days
Yes, bring back all the past . . .
let's put them all in rows again—so we can see who's last.
Let's label all the good ones
(the ones like you and me)
and make them into prefects—like prefects used to be.
We'll put them on the honours board
. . . as honours ought to be,
and write their names in burnished script—
for all the world to see.
We'll have them back in uniform,
we'll have them doff their caps,
and learn what manners really are
. . . for decent kind of chaps!
. . . So let's label all the good ones,
we'll call them 'A's and 'B's—
and we'll parcel up the useless ones
and call them 'C's and 'D's.
. . . We'll even have an 'E' lot!
. . . an 'F' and 'G' maybe!!
. . . so they can know they're useless,
. . . and not as good as me.

For we've got to have the stupid—
And we've got to have the poor
Because—

> if we don't have them . . .
> well . . . what are prefects for?

PETER DIXON

Exercise Book

Two and two four
four and four eight
eight and eight sixteen...
Once again! says the master
Two and two four
four and four eight
eight and eight sixteen.
But look! the lyre bird
high on the wing
the child sees it
the child hears it
the child calls it
Save me
play with me.
bird!
So the bird alights
and plays with the child
Two and two four...
Once again! says the master
and the child plays
and the bird plays too...
Four and four eight
eight and eight sixteen
and twice sixteen makes what?
Twice sixteen makes nothing
least of all thirty-two
anyhow

and off they go
For the child has hidden
The bird in his desk
and all the children
hear its song
and all the children
hear the music
and eight and eight in their turn
off they go
and four and four and two and two
in their turn fade away
and one and one make neither one nor two
but one by one off they go.
And the lyre-bird sings
and the child sings
and the master shouts
When you've quite finished playing the fool!
But all the children
Are listening to the music
And the walls of the classroom
quietly crumble.
The window panes turn
once more to sand
the ink is sea
the desk is trees
the chalk is cliffs
and the quill pen
a bird again.

PAUL DEHN

Timothy Winters

Timothy Winters comes to school
With eyes as wide as a football-pool,
Ears like bombs and teeth like splinters:
A blitz of a boy is Timothy Winters.

His belly is white, his neck is dark,
And his hair is an exclamation-mark.
His clothes are enough to scare a crow
And through his britches the blue winds blow.

When teacher talks he won't hear a word
And he shoots down dead the arithmetic-bird,
He licks the patterns off his plate
And he's not even heard of the Welfare State.

Timothy Winters has bloody feet
And he lives in a house on Suez Street,
He sleeps in a sack on the kitchen floor
And they say there aren't boys like him any more.

Old Man Winters likes his beer
And his missus ran off with a bombardier,
Grandma sits in the grate with a gin
And Timothy's dosed with an aspirin.

The Welfare Worker lies awake
But the law's as tricky as a ten-foot snake,
So Timothy Winters drinks his cup
And slowly goes on growing up.

At Morning Prayers the Master helves
For children less fortunate than ourselves,
And the loudest response in the room is when
Timothy Winters roars 'Amen!'

So come one angel, come on ten:
Timothy Winters says 'Amen
Amen amen amen amen.'
Timothy Winters, Lord,
                    Amen.

CHARLES CAUSLEY

154

A History Lesson

Kings
like golden gleams
made with a mirror on the wall.

A non-alcoholic pope,
knights without arms,
arms without knights.

The dead like so many strained noodles,
a pound of those fallen in battle,
two ounces of those who were executed,

several heads
like so many potatoes
shaken into a cap—

Geniuses conceived
by the mating of dates
are soaked up by the ceiling into infinity

to the sound of tinny thunder,
the rumble of bellies,
shouts of hurrah,

empires rise and fall
at a wave of the pointer,
the blood is blotted out—

And only one small boy,
who was not paying the least attention,
will ask
between two victorious wars:

And did it hurt in those days too?

MIROSLAV HOLUB
(*Trans. I. Milner and G. Theiner*)

In and out of school. In the few minutes before the bell for the end of afternoon school most people begin to feel restless. What things show this? What do you notice about other people's movements? What sounds are you aware of? Does your attention wander? Where?

What is your reaction and that of the rest of the class to the bell itself?

What are your feelings on getting out of school?

What are the *particular* sights and sounds which create the atmosphere of bustle and activity at the end of *your* school day?

Working in pairs, list all the things you can think of about the end of school. Then arrange the items into a description which catches the atmosphere. It might begin with the time of the final bell—'A quarter to four means: ....' and so on.

Performance. *Exercise Book* (p. 152) can be read aloud in groups. Decide which lines should be chanted together and which are best read by single voices. Rehearse your readings. You will probably have several different performances in the class.

—*Timothy Winters* (p. 154) is probably best shared out verse by verse among a group of three or four readers. See what you can do with the repeated 'Amen' at the end.

—*Oh bring back higher standards* (p. 150) is a sarcastic poem best performed in a rousing way by three voices. Rehearse it first by handing over to the next speaker at the start of each sentence. Then see if you can find better ways of sharing out the lines.

Sequel. Miroslav Holub's poem *A Boy's Head* (p. 141) imagines some of the strange and varied things that take up space in a boy's mind. List all the items that might occupy a girl's mind and write a sequel entitled *A Girl's Head*.

WAR

The Send-Off

Down the close, darkening lanes they sang their way
To the siding-shed,
And lined the train with faces grimly gay.

Their breasts were stuck all white with wreath and spray
As men's are, dead.

Dull porters watched them, and a casual tramp
Stood staring hard,
Sorry to miss them from the upland camp.
Then, unmoved, signals nodded, and a lamp
Winked to the guard.

So secretly, like wrongs hushed-up, they went.
They were not ours:
We never heard to which front these were sent.

Nor there if they yet mock what women meant
Who gave them flowers.

Shall they return to beatings of great bells
In wild train-loads?
A few, a few, too few for drums and yells,
May creep back, silent, to village wells
Up half-known roads.

WILFRED OWEN

The Sentry

We'd found an old Boche dug-out, and he knew,
And gave us hell, for shell on frantic shell
Hammered on top, but never quite burst through.
Rain, guttering down in waterfalls of slime
Kept slush waist-high that, rising hour by hour,
Choked up the steps too thick with clay to climb.
What murk of air remained stank old, and sour
With fumes of whizz-bangs, and the smell of men
Who'd lived there years, and left their curse in the den,
If not their corpses . . .

> There we herded from the blast
Of whizz-bangs, but one found our door at last,—
Buffeting eyes and breath, snuffing the candles.
And thud! flump! thud! down the steep steps came
    thumping
And splashing in the flood, deluging muck—
The sentry's body; then, his rifle, handles
Of old Boche bombs, and mud in ruck on ruck.
We dredged him up, for killed, until he whined
'O sir, my eyes—I'm blind—I'm blind, I'm blind!'
Coaxing, I held a flame against his lids
And said if he could see the least blurred light
He was not blind; in time he'd get all right.
'I can't,' he sobbed. Eyeballs, huge-bulged like squids',
Watch my dreams still; but I forgot him there
In posting next for duty, and sending a scout
To beg a stretcher somewhere, and floundering about
To other posts under the shrieking air.

Those other wretches, how they bled and spewed,
And one who would have drowned himself for good,—
I try not to remember these things now.
Let dread hark back for one word only: how
Half listening to that sentry's moans and jumps,
And the wild chattering of his broken teeth,
Renewed most horribly whenever crumps
Pummelled the roof and slogged the air beneath—
Through the dense din, I say, we heard him shout
'I see your lights!' But ours had long died out.

WILFRED OWEN

159

The Man He Killed

'Had he and I but met
    By some old ancient inn,
We should have sat us down to wet
    Right many a nipperkin![1]   [1] beer-mug

'But ranged as infantry,
    And staring face to face,
I shot at him as he at me,
    And killed him in his place.

'I shot him dead because—
    Because he was my foe,
Just so: my foe of course he was;
    That's clear enough; although

'He thought he'd list, perhaps,
    Off hand like—just as I—
Was out of work—had sold his traps—
    No other reason why.

'Yes; quaint and curious war is!
    You shoot a fellow down
You'd treat if met where any bar is,
    Or help to half-a-crown.'

                            THOMAS HARDY

160

Attack

At dawn the ridge emerges massed and dun
In the wild purple of the glow'ring sun,
Smouldering through spouts of drifting smoke that shroud
The menacing scarred slope; and, one by one,
Tanks creep and topple forward to the wire.
The barrage roars and lifts. Then, clumsily bowed
With bombs and guns and shovels and battle-gear,
Men jostle and climb to meet the bristling fire.
Lines of grey, muttering faces, masked with fear,
They leave their trenches, going over the top,
While time ticks blank and busy on their wrists,
And hope, with furtive eyes and grappling fists,
Flounders in mud. O Jesus, make it stop!

SIEGFRIED SASSOON

Counter-Attack

We'd gained our first objective hours before
While dawn broke like a face with blinking eyes,
Pallid, unshaved and thirsty, blind with smoke.
Things seemed alright at first. We held their line,
With bombers posted, Lewis guns well placed,
And clink of shovels deepening the shallow trench.
  The place was rotten with dead; green clumsy legs
  High-booted, sprawled and grovelled along the saps,
  And trunks, face downward, in the sucking mud,
  Wallowed like trodden sand-bags loosely filled;
  And naked sodden buttocks, mats of hair,
  Bulged, clotted heads slept in the plastering slime.
  And then the rain began—the jolly old rain!

A yawning soldier knelt against the bank,
Staring across the morning blear with fog;
He wondered when the Allemands would get busy;
And then, of course, they started with five-nines
Traversing, sure as fate, and never a dud.

Mute in the clamour of shells he watched them burst
Spouting dark earth and wire with gusts from hell,
While posturing giants dissolved in drifts of smoke.
He crouched and flinched, dizzy with galloping fear,
Sick for escape—loathing the strangled horror
And butchered, frantic gestures of the dead.

An officer came blundering down the trench:
'Stand-to and man the fire-step!' On he went . . .
Gasping and bawling, 'Fire-step . . . counter-attack!'
    Then the haze lifted. Bombing on the right
    Down the old sap: machine-guns on the left;
    And stumbling figures looming out in front.
    'O Christ, they're coming at us!' Bullets spat,
And he remembered his rifle . . . rapid fire . . .
And started blazing wildly . . . then a bang
Crumpled and spun him sideways, knocked him out
To grunt and wriggle: none heeded him; he choked
And fought the flapping veils of smothering gloom,
Lost in a blurred confusion of yells and groans . . .
Down, and down, and down, he sank and drowned,
Bleeding to death. The counter-attack had failed.

SIEGFRIED SASSOON

Wirers

'Pass it along, the wiring party's going out'—
And yawning sentries mumble, 'Wirers going out.'
Unravelling; twisting; hammering stakes with muffled thud,
They toil with stealthy haste and anger in their blood.

The Boche sends up a flare. Black forms stand rigid there,
Stock-still like posts; then darkness, and the clumsy ghosts
Stride hither and thither, whispering, tripped by
   clutching snare
Of snags and tangles.
              Ghastly dawn with vaporous coasts
Gleams desolate along the sky, night's misery ended.

Young Hughes was badly hit; I heard him carried away,
Moaning at every lurch; no doubt he'll die today.
But *we* can say the front-line wire's been safely mended.

SIEGFRIED SASSOON

The Battle

Helmet and rifle, pack and overcoat
Marched through a forest. Somewhere up ahead
Guns thudded. Like the circle of a throat
The night on every side was turning red.

They halted and they dug. They sank like moles
Into the clammy earth between the trees.
And soon the sentries, standing in their holes,
Felt the first snow. Their feet began to freeze.

At dawn the first shell landed with a crack.
Then shells and bullets swept the icy woods.
This lasted many days. The snow was black.
The corpses stiffened in their scarlet hoods.

Most clearly of that battle I remember
The tiredness in eyes, how hands looked thin
Around a cigarette, and the bright ember
Would pulse with all the life there was within.

LOUIS SIMPSON

Old Soldier

A dream of battle on a windy night
Has wakened him. The shadows move once more
With rumours of alarm. He sees the height
And helmet of his terror in the door.

The guns reverberate; a livid arc
From sky to sky lightens the windowpanes
And all his room. The clock ticks in the dark;
A cool wind stirs the curtains, and it rains.

He lies remembering: 'That's how it was . . .'
And smiles, and drifts into a youthful sleep
Without a care. His life is all he has,
And that is given to the guards to keep.

LOUIS SIMPSON

Night Patrol

We sail at dusk. The red moon,
Rising in a paper lantern, sets fire
To the water, the black headland disappears,
Sullen in shadow, clenched like a paw.

The docks grow flat, rubbered with mist.
Cranes, like tall drunks, hang
Over the railway. The unloading of coal
Continues under blue arc-lights.

Turning south, the moon like a rouged face
Between masts, the knotted aerials swing
Taut against the horizon, the bag
Of sea crumpled in the spray-flecked blackness.

Towards midnight the cold stars, high
Over Europe, freeze on the sky,
Stigmata above the flickering lights
Of Holland. Flashes of gunfire

Lick out over meditative coastlines, betraying
The stillness. Taking up position, night falls
Exhausted about us. The wakes
Of gunboats sew the green dark with speed.

From Dunkirk red flames open fanwise
In spokes of light; like the rising moon
Setting fire to the sky, the remote
Image of death burns on the water.

The slow muffle of hours. Clouds grow visible.
Altering course the moon congeals on a new
Bearing. Northwards again, and Europe recedes
With the first sharp splinters of dawn.

The orange sky lies over the harbour,
Derricks and pylons like scarecrows
Black in the early light. And minesweepers
Pass us, moving out slowly to the North Sea.

ALAN ROSS

Air Raid across the Bay at Plymouth

I
Above the whispering sea
And waiting rocks of black coast,
Across the bay, the searchlight beams
Swing and swing back across the sky.

Their ends fuse in a cone of light
Held for a bright instant up
Until they break away again
Smashing that image like a cup.

II
Delicate aluminium girders
Project phantom aerial masts
Swaying crane and derrick
Above the sea's just lifting deck.

III
Triangles, parallels, parallelograms,
Experiment with hypotheses
On the blackboard sky,
Seeking that X
Where the enemy is met.
Two beams cross
To chalk his cross.

IV
A sound, sounding ragged, unseen
Is chased by two swords of light.
A thud. An instant when the whole night gleams.
Gold sequins shake out of a black-silk screen.

V
Jacob ladders slant
Up to the god of war
Who, from his heaven-high car,
Unloads upon a star
A destroying star.

Round the coast, the waves
Chuckle between rocks.
In the fields the corn
Sways, with metallic clicks.
Man hammers nails in Man,
High on his crucifix.

STEPHEN SPENDER

Grass

Pile the bodies high at Austerlitz and Waterloo.
Shovel them under and let me work—
    I am the grass; I cover all.

And pile them high at Gettysburg
And pile them high at Ypres and Verdun.
Shovel them under and let me work.
Two years, ten years, and passengers ask the conductor:
    What place is this?
    Where are we now?

    I am the grass.
    Let me work.

CARL SANDBURG

The Fly

She sat on a willow-trunk
watching
part of the battle of Crécy,
the shouts
the gasps,
the groans,
the tramping and the tumbling.

During the fourteenth charge
of the French cavalry
she mated
with a brown-eyed male fly
from Vadincourt.

She rubbed her legs together
as she sat on a disembowelled horse
meditating
on the immortality of flies.

With relief she alighted
on the blue tongue
of the Duke of Clervaux.

When silence settled
and only the whisper of decay
softly circled the bodies

and only
a few arms and legs
still twitched jerkily under the trees,

she began to lay her eggs
on the single eye
of Johann Uhr,
the Royal Armourer.

And thus it was
that she was eaten by a swift
fleeing
from the fires of Estrées.

MIROSLAV HOLUB
(Trans. I. Milner and G. Theiner)

Museum of Artillery at Woolwich

Guns;
thick curves
of polished sunlight,
small boys
stroke the skin of war.

They mouth endearments,
almost feel
each weapon flex its
metal spine;
wiped clean of ghosts
and blood
the shine is sensuous.

The monument above
their heads
has sugared cherubs
blowing plump kisses
over cannon
cut from marble ice.

Death is sinuously forged;
thin blades
of ancient swords excite
desire for thrust
and shape.

Tin soldiers boxed in glass,
die for a coin
in-a-slot
among red paint
and cotton-buds of smoke.

The children laugh;
buy postcards at the door.

ISOBEL THRILLING

Air Raid

After the bedtime story,
a siren
cracked open my head.
We whispered
as if the planes could
hear our voices.

The shelter was bricked
in darkness
hung with incomplete faces,
the side of a nose,
a cheek-bone,
a chin,
the whites of our eyes.

I sat on the wooden slats
and hugged my doll.
I knew
she was afraid,
could feel her terror
cradled in
my arms like a bomb.

ISOBEL THRILLING

1915

Those mothers: how could they bear it?
Did they tear up the yellowing snapshots:

That picnic when he fell into the pond;
The outing with the Sunday school
(Scowling, mutinous, in the second row);
The cricket match; more groups, and last of all,
His first leave.
    He's almost finished, here,
With childish things.

Fresh-faced, wide-eyed he turns. He's on his way
To the muddy abattoir.

Lucky for us, whose children survive to mortgages
And greyness.

CONNIE BENSLEY

Mother the Wardrobe is Full of Infantrymen

mother the wardrobe is full of infantrymen
i did i asked them
but they snarled saying it was a mans life

mother there is a centurion tank in the parlour
i did i asked the officer
but he laughed saying 'Queens regulations'
(piano was out of tune anyway)

mother polish your identity bracelet
there is a mushroom cloud in the backgarden
i did i tried to bring in the cat
but it simply came to pieces in my hand
i did i tried to whitewash the windows
but there weren't any
i did i tried to hide under the stairs
but i couldn't get in for civil defence leaders
i did i tried ringing candid camera
but they crossed their hearts

i went for a policeman but they were looting the town
i went out for a fire engine but they were all upside down
i went for a priest but they were all on their knees
mother don't just lie there say something please
mother don't just lie there say something please

ROGER McGOUGH

Bang

When the goodies are all gone
what shall we do
with the old brown bag of an earth
but blow it up—BANG

Crumpled brown paper bag
scuttling along
the desolate white
lanes of the universe

GERDA MEYER

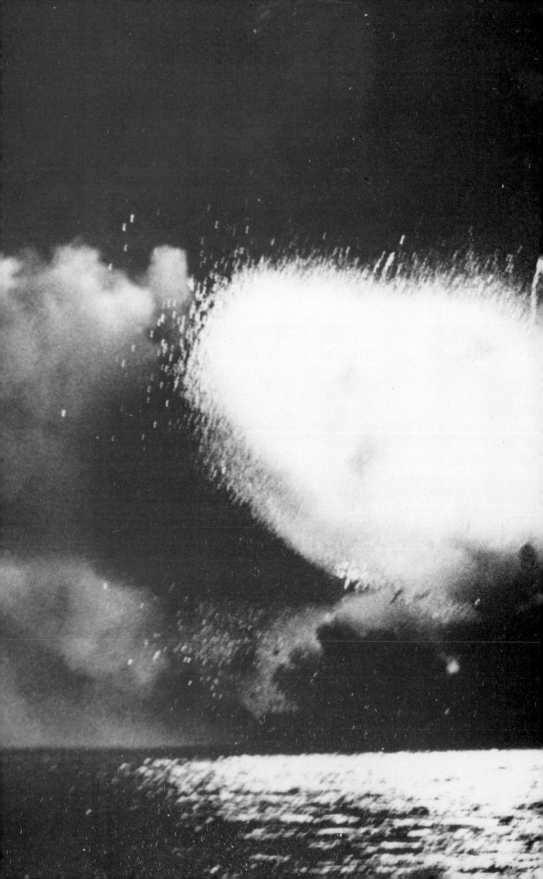

Three Weeks to Argentina

Shall I wave my little
Union Jack?
Shall I go all out for
a big attack?
Shall I sing: 'My country
right or wrong!'?
Shall I rattle out a
sabre song?

Or shall I write of
sailor boys
deep in the sea, that can
make no noise?
Or of feckless, careless
young marines
missed by the girls
and the wet canteens?

It's hard for an old man,
who's seen wars,
to welcome that devil
and his claws.

They reach from the ocean,
clash in the sky,
make the earth into
a shepherd's pie.

Professionals love it,
the admirals all,
a chance to show that they're
on the ball.
Newsmen like it,
because it's news—
but fathers and mothers
have different views.

17 April 1982

GAVIN EWART

None of you will have experienced a war, yet none of you will have escaped secondhand contact with wars through television and newspapers. Some of you will be keen on war stories and, either through books or films, will know about a few of the more glamorous exploits and, maybe, something of the suffering of the two world wars. The fascination which the subject of war has for many people lies, perhaps, in the mixture of excitement and horror: it is an extreme situation which produces extreme emotions. The frequency with which sharp-eyed cameramen bring pictures of the latest slaughters into everyone's living-room gives us a dangerous familiarity with the horrors of war: dangerous, because with television or press pictures we are, except on rare occasions, uninvolved in what is happening. A passing feeling of 'how dreadful', a temporary concern for those who suffer—these are the reactions that we usually muster—for we have seen it so often before and it is happening so far away. It has nothing to do with us. Real wars take their place as unreal fictions alongside the Western and the thriller.

The value of reading the poems we have printed here and in attempting to put down your own thoughts and feelings about war is partly that these things act as correctives to this danger: war becomes a fact we have to face. We can attempt to come to terms with this terrible subject in various ways.

Taped interview. You are an interviewer, perhaps for a children's TV or radio programme, and you decide to talk to your grandparents or other relatives about how the Second World War affected them. Some may have been on active service abroad but most people will have seen a different side to war: rationbooks . . . queues for food, toys, or clothing . . . gas-masks . . . the Home Guard . . . blackout . . . air-raid sirens . . . searchlights . . . air-raid shelters . . . bombed areas . . . evacuation . . . the blitz . . . 'Lord Haw-Haw'. Working in pairs, prepare a list of questions you want to ask (some may be suggested by the ideas above) and then, individually, arrange to tape record your interview. Extracts from the tapes can be played back, perhaps in groups, as part of your work on this theme.

Phrase collage. The group of First World War poems by Owen and Sassoon (pp. 157–166) will give you some insight into the world of trench warfare. Hear these poems read aloud. Then read them through quietly to yourself or in pairs and, as you do so, make a note of particular lines or phrases that seem to you to capture the feeling of warfare. When you have your collection, arrange and illustrate the words on a single sheet of paper as a 'war collage'.

Pictures into poems

—The painting *Lens Bombed* (p. 163) shows the nightmare reality of civilian bombing. It dates from the First World War when planes were first used in this way.

—*Paths of Glory* (pp. 164–165) pictures the battlefield in the same war.

—*The Bombed House* (p. 174) was drawn by a 16 year old at school during the Second World War.

—Soldiers in action (p. 167) shows two American servicemen in the Korean War.

Talk in pairs about the pictures and note down any *details* that seem to you to catch the feelings of wartime—the expression on a face, the movement or position of the figures, the setting . . . Write about *one* of these details as a sort of caption to the picture. The pictures and captions could then be arranged as a class display.

Weapons. Most of you, at one time or another, will have seen weapons of war on show. Some of you will have been to air displays and seen fighter planes, bombers, perhaps even guided missiles; others of you may have seen tanks on manoeuvres or warships and submarines in port.

Perhaps you could describe one of these weapons in detail and think about its purpose.

Acknowledgments

The editors and publishers would like to thank the copyright holders mentioned in the list below for their kind permission to reproduce copyright material by the following poets:

Fleur Adcock: 'A Game', reprinted from Fleur Adcock's *Selected Poems* (1983) by permission of Oxford University Press.

John Agard: 'Rainbow Child' and 'Child Waiting', by permission of the author Connie Bensley: '1915' from *Moving In*, Peterloo Poets, 1984, by permission of the author.

John Betjeman' Slough' from *Collected Poems*, John Murray Ltd.

Elizabeth Bishop: 'The Fish' from *Selected Poems*, Chatto and Windus Ltd.

Jorges Luis Borges: First stanza of 'Tankas' from *The Book of Sand* and *The Gold of the Tigers*, translated by Norman Thomas di Giovanni and Alastair Reid, Penguin Books, 1979, copyright © Emence Editores, sa, Buenos Aires, 1972, 1975, English translation copyright © Alastair Reid, 1976, 1977, 1979, page 103. Reproduced by permission of Penguin Books Ltd and E. P. Dutton, a division of NAL Penguin Inc.

William Carlos Williams: 'A Negro Woman' from *Pictures from Breughel*, MacGibbon & Kee Ltd.

Charles Causley: 'Timothy Winters' from *Union Street*, Rupert Hart-Davis, and 'The Ballad of Charlotte Dymond' from *Collected Poems*, published by Macmillan, reproduced by permission of David Higham Associates Ltd.

Wendy Cope: 'Tich Miller' from *Making Cocoa for Kingsley Amis*, by permission of Faber & Faber Ltd.

Hart Crane: 'March' from *The Complete Poems and Selected Letters and Prose*, by permission of Oxford University Press.

Martyn Crucefix: 'Light Poem', reprinted by permission of the author.

Paul Dehn: 'Exercise Book' from *The Fern on the Rock*, copyright © 1965 (from the French of Jacques Prévert), Hamish Hamilton, London.

Walter de la Mare: 'Ice' reprinted by permission of The Literary Trustees of Walter de la Mare and the Society of Authors as their representative.

Emily Dickinson: 'A Bird Came Down the Walk', reprinted by permission of the publishers and the Trustees of Amherst College from Thomas H. Johnson, Editor, *The Poems of Emily Dickinson*, Cambridge, Mass.: The Belknap Press of Harvard University Press, copyright © 1951, 1955, by The President and Fellows of Harvard College.

Peter Dixon: 'Oh Bring Back Higher Standards'.

Dominic Dowell: 'Tree', Fitzjohn's School.

T. S. Eliot: extract from 'The Love Song of J. Alfred Prufrock; from *The Collected Poems of T. S. Eliot*, Faber & Faber Ltd.

Gavin Ewart: 'Three Weeks to Argentina' from *The Young Pobble's Guide to his Toes*, by permission of Century Hutchinson Ltd.

Vicki Feaver: 'The Round Pond' and 'Slow Reader', by permission of the author.

Robert Frost: 'Nothing Gold can Stay' and 'The Runaway' from *The Complete Poems of Robert Frost*, Jonathan Cape Ltd and Holt, Rinehart and Winston Inc.

Robert Graves: 'Welsh Incident' from *Collected Poems*, 1975, by permission of A. P. Watt Ltd on behalf of the Executors of the Estate of Robert Graves.

Thom Gunn: 'Considering the Snail' from *My Sad Captains*, Faber & Faber Ltd.

Thomas Hardy: 'The Man he Killed' from *Collected Poems by Thomas Hardy*, by permission of the Trustees of the Hardy Estate and Macmillan & Co. Ltd.

Seamus Heaney: 'Cow in Calf', 'Blackberry-Picking', 'An Advancement of Learning' and extracts from 'Death of a Naturalist', 'Waterfall' and 'Docker' from *Death of a Naturalist*, Faber & Faber Ltd; 'Rookery', *The Listener*; 'May Day', New Statesman.

H. G. Henderson: 'The Poor Man's Son', 'The Weeping Willow', 'A Wish', 'The Cuckoo's Song', 'City People' and 'The Dragonfly' from *An Introduction to Haiku* by Harold G. Henderson, copyright © 1958 by Harold G. Henderson, reprinted by permission of Doubleday & Company Inc.

Phoebe Hesketh: 'Going Away and Returning' and 'Cats' from *Prayer for the Sun*, Rupert Hart-Davis Ltd.

Miroslav Holub: 'In the Microscope' from *Penguin Selected Poems*, translated by I. Milner and G. Theiner, Penguin Books Ltd.

Ted Hughes: 'Wind' and 'October Dawn' from *The Hawk in the Rain*; 'View of a Pig' and 'To Paint a Waterlily' from *Lupercal*; 'Full Moon and Little Frieda' from *Wodwo*; an extract from 'Mooses' from *Under the North Star*, and 'The Rooster' from *What is the Truth?*, Faber & Faber Ltd.

Evan Jones: 'Lament of the Banana Man' from *Young Commonwealth Poets*, reprinted by permission of William Heinemann Ltd.

James Kirkup: 'Tea in a Spaceship' and 'Earthquake', by permission of the author.

Günter Kunert: 'Film Put in Backwards' from *East German Poetry*, ed. Michael Hamburger, this translation by permission of Christopher Middleton.

D. H. Lawrence: 'The Optimist', 'Last Lesson in the Afternoon' and extracts from 'The Storm in the Black Forest', 'Snake', 'Fish' and 'Kangaroo' from *The Complete Poems of D. H. Lawrence*, Laurence Pollinger Ltd and the Estate of the late Mrs Frieda Lawrence.

Liz Lochhead: 'Poem for my Sister' and 'The Choosing' from *Dreaming Frankenstein and Collected Poems*, Polygon.

Edward Lucie-Smith: 'The Lesson' from *A Tropical Childhood and Other Poems*, by permission of Oxford University Press.

Roger McGough: 'The Commission', 'Out and About the Lads' and 'Smithereens' from *In the Glassroom*, 'The Fight of the Year' from *Watchwords*, reprinted by permission of Jonathan Cape Ltd; 'Mother the Wardrobe is full of Infantrymen' from *Modern Poets 10*, Penguin Books Ltd, reprinted by permission of A. D. Peters & Co. Ltd.

Louis MacNiece: 'Corner Seat', 'Reflections' and 'Under the Mountain' from *The Collected Poems of Louis MacNeice*, reprinted by permission of Faber & Faber Ltd.

Gerda Mayer: 'BANG' from *Monkey on the Analyst's Couch*, published by Ceolfrith Press, and '529 1983' from *The Knockabout Show*, by permission of the author.

Spike Milligan: 'Kangaroo-Kangaroo!' from *Unspun Socks from a Chicken's Laundry*, Michael Joseph Ltd.

Edwin Morgan: 'An Island in the City' from *Poems of Thirty Years*, 1982, by permission of Carcanet Press.

A. Moritake: 'Fallen Flower' from *Penguin Book of Japanese Verse*, translated by G. Bownas and A. Thwaite, Penguin Books Ltd.

Ogden Nash: 'Lather As You Go' from *Family Reunion*, J. M. Dent and Sons Ltd.

183

Grace Nichols: 'Waiting for Thelma's Daughter' and 'Island Man', by permission of the author.
Norman Nicholson: 'From a Boat at Coniston', 'The Motion of the Earth' and an extract from 'Mountain Limestone' all from *The Pot Geranium*, by permission of Faber & Faber Ltd.
Gareth Owen: 'Street Boy' from *Salford Road*, and 'Space Shot' and 'Typewriting Class' from *Song of the City*, by permission of Collins Publishers.
Wilfred Owen: 'The Send Off' and 'The Sentry' from *The Collected Poems of Wilfred Owen*, Mr Harold Owen and Chatto and Windus Ltd.
Stef Pixner: 'Term Begins Again' from *Sawdust and White Spirit*, by permission of Virago Press Ltd.
Sylvia Plath: 'Mushrooms' from *The Colossus* by courtesy of Miss Olwyn Hughes.
Po Chu'I: 'The Red Cockatoo' from *170 Chinese Poems*, translated by Arthur Waley, Constable Publishers.
Ezra Pound: 'In a Station of the Metro' and 'Fan Piece for her Imperial Lord' from *Collected Shorter Poems*, by permission of Faber & Faber Ltd.
Jacques Prévert: 'To Paint the Portrait of a Bird' from *Paroles*, translated by Lawrence Ferlinghetti, Penguin Books Ltd.
Peter Redgrove: 'Thirteen Ways of Looking at a Blackboard' from *The Collected and Other Poems*, Routledge and Kegan Paul Plc.
Theodore Roethke: 'Flower Dump' from *Words for the Wind*, Martin Secker & Warburg.
Alan Ross: 'Night Patrol' from *Poems 1942–67*, Eyre & Spottiswoode (Publishers) Ltd.
George Rostrevor Hamilton: 'Hawk' from *Collected Poems and Epigrams*, William Heinemann Ltd.
Siegfried Sassoon: 'Wirers', 'Counter-Attack' and 'Attack' from *Collected Poems*, Mr George Sassoon, executor of the Estate of the late Siegfried Sassoon.
Louis Simpson: 'Old Soldier' from *A Dream of Governors* by Louis Simpson, copyright © 1959 by Louis Simpson, reprinted by permission of Wesleyan University Press; 'The Battle', reprinted by permission of Charles Scribner's Sons from *Good News of Death and Other Poems* by Louis Simpson, copyright © 1955 Louis Simpson (*Poets of Today II*).
Wole Soyinka: 'Season' from *Modern Poetry from Africa*, by courtesy of Mrs O. Soyinka.
Stephen Spender: 'Air Raid Across the Bay at Plymouth' from *Collected Poems*, Faber & Faber Ltd.
L. A. G. Strong: 'Matthew Bird' from *The Body's Imperfection*, Methuen & Co. Ltd.
May Swenson: 'Water Picture' copyright © 1965 May Swenson, first published in *The New Yorker*, reprinted by permission of Charles Scribner's Sons from *To Mix With Time* by May Swenson.
A. S. J. Tessimond: 'Cats' from *Selection*, Putnam & Co. Ltd and Hubert Nicholson, literary executor to the late A. S. J. Tessimond. Edward Thomas: 'Cock-Crow' from *Selected Poems*, Mrs Myfanwy Thomas.
Anthony Thwaite: 'The Pond' from *The Stones of Emptiness*, by permission of Oxford University Press
Kenneth Yasuda: 'The Mississippi River' from *A Pepper Pod: Haiku Samples*, Charles E. Tuttle Co. Inc. of Tokyo, Japan.
Benjamin Zephaniah: 'I Love Me Mudder (Mother)' from *The Dread Affair*, Arena, an imprint of Century Hutchinson.

Every effort has been made to trace the copyright holders of the following poems:

W. Stevens: 'Someone Puts a Pineapple Together' (7 line extract).
Isobel Thrilling: 'Kitten in a Tree', 'Advice to a Teenage Daughter', 'Museum of Artillery at Woolwich' and 'Air Raid'.

The editors and publishers would also like to thank the following for permission to reproduce illustrations:

The Natural History Photographic Agency (pp. 11, 15, 17, 49, 131, 157); Barnaby's Picture Library (pp. 90, 109, 114); John and Penny Hubley (p. 22); The Mansell Collection: 'The Cornfield' by Constable (pp. 23 and 24); T. W. Lomax (p. 25); Kunsthistorisches Museum, Vienna: 'Winter' and 'Spring' by Arcimboldo (pp. 30, 104) and detail from 'Hunters in the Snow' by Bruegel (p. 113); Michael Rothenstein: 'The Cockerel' (p. 38); the Electricity Council (Laurie Melia) (p. 43); The British Museum: 'Storm at Shono' by Hokusai (pp. 45–6); Mogens Carrebye: 'Reflection of trees in an old man's glasses' from the Beatles' film *The Fool on the Hill* (pp. 58–9); Sally and Richard Greenhill (pp. 68 and 145); Tomio Seike: 'Lipstick' (p. 73); John Warwicker (p. 75); Popperfoto (pp. 87, 168–9, 177); John Hillelson Agency (pp. 89, 97); Mt Wilson and Palomar Observations: 'Moon, Region of Copernicus' (p. 95); Berks and Bucks Observer (p. 100); The Guardian (p. 124); Imperial War Museum (p. 158) and also 'Paths of Glory' by Nevinson (p. 163); Philadelphia Museum of Art: 'Lens Bombed' by Otto Dix (pp. 164–5); Penguin Books, *Children as Artists* by R. R. Tomlinson (p. 174); The Press Association (pp. 178–9).

Every effort has been made to trace the copyright holders of 'A Cage and its Bird' by Maria Teresa Lazzaroni (p. 51).